THE HERMENEUTIC OF ERASMUS

BASEL STUDIES OF THEOLOGY

edited by the Faculty of Theology, Basel

No. 2

THE HERMENEUTIC
OF ERASMUS

by

JOHN WILLIAM ALDRIDGE

JOHN KNOX PRESS · RICHMOND (VIRGINIA)

Library of Congress Catalog Card Number: 66 - 20 331
Joint publication by
EVZ-Verlag, Zürich, and John Knox Press, Richmond, Virginia
© EVZ-Verlag, Zürich, 1966

Printed by Walter Pieper, Würzburg
Printed in Germany

CONTENTS

INTRODUCTION

Kurt Aland has remarked that "die Frage der rechten Auslegung der Schrift ist das Thema der Theologie von heute" [1], and if we take note of the titles of the many books of recent publication, with either the word 'hermeneutic' or 'interpretation' in the title, then we can surmise that this statement of Aland's has certain validity.

To develop the hermeneutic of Erasmus will not solve the current hermeneutical debate, but it will give some insight concerning the present day discussion and it will enable us to see the problem more clearly.

The importance of developing the hermeneutic of Erasmus will therefore have two aspects. The first lies in the hermeneutic itself, where we shall see that in many ways Erasmus' principles of interpretation have validity today. The second aspect is the relation of Erasmus' hermeneutic to his times, particularly to Luther, and therefore the Reformation. Even though Erasmus differs from the Reformation hermeneutic, he gives impetus to it.

Erasmus represents a departure from the typical Middle Age hermeneutic, not so much in substance as in method. But Erasmus also differs from the Reformation theory of interpretation. How does he differ from these two methods, and can we see a connecting thread here? These and other questions will occupy our attention. For the importance of the hermeneutic of Erasmus lies not only in stating it, but also in showing its particular value to the period in which Erasmus lived.

Our task is theological rather than historical. Still we must keep the historical man and his times in view in order to be able to grasp the theological significance of his hermeneutic. Therefore our aim is to develop Erasmus' theory of interpretation in the manner and sequence that he himself developed it.

---

[1] *Kirchengeschichtliche Entwürfe*, Berlin, 1960. p. 395.

Chapter I

AD FONTES

To develop the hermeneutic of Erasmus it is essential to begin with *ad fontes*, for it is from this starting point that Erasmus develops his own hermeneutic. The method by which Erasmus employs *ad fontes* determines his basic dissimilarity with the Middle Age method of interpretation. *Ad fontes* is also to become both the point of contact and the point of divergence between Erasmus and the Reformers.

Erasmus was a Renaissance man and a product of that movement. As the word renaissance implies rebirth, it follows that Erasmus, with the other men of that movement, was greatly interested in a rebirth of antiquity. But Erasmus was also one of the leaders in making the Renaissance, and its counterpart, Humanism, a Christian movement. Therefore he envisioned not only a rebirth of antiquity as such, but moreover a rebirth of man in a Christian setting, a spiritual Renaissance [1] that was to be the basis and the underlying principle behind this rebirth of antiquity. This new age was to be an age combining the very best of the classical and the Christian world, a classical world moulded into a Christian pattern, a Christianized classical world.

The means by which this renaissance is accomplished is through a genuine return to the sources. The formula is simple: A dedicated study of the sources produces an authentic rebirth.

So far we have been speaking in generalities. Specifically what is the importance of the term *ad fontes* to Erasmus? It is from this starting point that Erasmus develops his hermeneutic. It is from this starting point that Erasmus moves away from the typically Renaissance and Humanistic view of his early life until he, through

---

1) "Paraclesis", Holborn, 145.5. "Quid autem aliud est Christi philosophia quam ipse *renascentiam* vocat, quam instauratio bene conditae naturae?" This is an example of Erasmus' Christian Humanistic *Bildung* of a true Renaissance.
Cf. Allen, 337.327. "Ambiunt in senatu theologorum aliquid esse, et verentur ne, si *renascantur* bonae litterae et si resipiscat mundus, videantur nihil scisse, qui antehac vulgo nihil nescire videbantur."

a dedicated study of the sources, puts forth his own unique concepts that are to propel him from one arena directly into another; i. e., from the Renaissance, of which he was king, into the Reformation, where every concept he held dear was challenged.

From the very beginning Erasmus was always interested in the sources. Even in so early a work as *Anti Barbarorum Liber*, in which he argues passionately that a scholarly approach necessarily begins at the sources [2], Erasmus attaches significant importance to source study. There is never any deviation in the importance of the sources. This remained constant, but there is development concerning which source is the most important; a development from the sources to a primary source.

Erasmus began his early life as a thorough-going Renaissance scholar with all the trimmings: the flowery style, the hero worship, the interest in classical mythology, the over-numerous quotes from the classics, and a total emersion in the ideas of antiquity [3]. But he was to move very definitely toward a Christian Humanism, even to the point that he could be classified under the Renaissance movement only with a certain reservation; that is, that classical studies rather than being the *summum bonum* of literature, must be adapted or made serviceable to Christianity [4]. For Erasmus found the deepest meaning of cultured literature not in its intrinsic value but in its benefits to theology.

Following his first visit to England in the years 1499—1500, a definite change takes place in Erasmus' thinking. Not a change in the importance of using the sources, because from start to finish there is nothing that takes precedence over this, but a change toward the Holy Scripture as the chief source.

This change occurs primarily under the influence of John Colet, who had been lecturing on the Pauline Epistles at Oxford since 1496. Colet's father had twice been Lord-Mayor of London and Colet had studied in France and Italy. He was widely read and had

---

2) *Anti Barbarorum Liber,* Gouda Manuscript, p. 10. "Audi magnifice contemptor, prius literas disce, postea contemne."

3) One needs only to read the early epistles of Erasmus to see his interest in the Renaissance and its influence on his letters. See particularly Allen, 20.89 f., in which Erasmus lists a wide variety of the writers and poets of antiquity as a study guide for his friend, Cornelius Gerard.

4) Allen, 2136.185. "Prouexi linguas ac politiores litteras, magno rei theologicae bono."

a good knowledge of the Church Fathers. Though he possessed an insufficient knowledge of Greek, he still strove for the original meaning of the Biblical text in his lectures.

Erasmus was not only enthusiastic over the approach of Colet, but also encouraged by it. It was an approach that Erasmus had been yearning to hear expounded, since his adventures in the University of Paris had more than whetted his appetite for someone more interested in original meanings of authors than in disputations. Moreover Colet's lectures led to a direct contact with an animated form of Biblical exegesis. This awakened interest in the Scriptures was to become one of the major turning points in Erasmus' life, and the close friendship he formed with Colet supplemented and enlarged what he was able to gather from the classroom. From his conversations with Colet was to arise his first theological writing, a small essay on the anxiety, fear and sadness of Jesus in the garden of Gethsemane [5]. It is not a purely theological discussion, for he included two mythological examples, but in this small work we discern a theological orientation taking shape.

This is not to say that Erasmus' humanistic bent was displaced once and for all, for still to come forth from his pen was the *Moria Encomiom*. This work is filled with the most biting satire, although even here we find evidence of a desire for Christian reform, a reform that is based on the Scriptures as the source [6]. Nevertheless, one of Erasmus' finest works was to come immediately following his first visit to England, *Enchiridion Militis Christiani* [7]. In this

---

5) Allen, *Epistles*, 108—111.

6) *Moria Encomiom*, LB iv, 468 c. "At interim ipsi felicissimi sibi placent, imo plaudunt, adeo ut his suavissimis naeniis, nocte dieque occupatis, ne tantulum quidem otii supersit ut Euangelium, aut Paulinas Epistolas vel semel liceat evolvere."

Ibid., LB iv, 465 c. "Iam has subtissimus subtilitates subtiliores etiam reddunt tot scholasticorum viae, ut citius e labyrinthis temet explices, quam ex involucris Realium, Nominalium, Thomistarum, Albertistarum, Occanistarum, Scotistarum, et nondum omneis dixi, sed praecipuas dumtaxat. In quibus omnibus tantum est eruditionis tantum difficultatis, ut existimem ipsis Apostolis alio spiritu opus fore, si cogantur hisce de rebus cum hoc novo Theologrum genere conserere manus."

7) It is interesting to note that this work on piety helped to satisfy the other side of Erasmus' nature, the deep-rooted ethical and pietistic side, which he learned while a young schoolboy at Deventer for the Brothers of the Common Life and their *Devotio Moderna*, which was theologically based to a large extent on the work, *De imitatione Christi*. Cf. *Ratio ... Ad Veram*

work we see more of the mature Erasmus, as he states that he has used the best of ancient literature that he might best adorn the Temple of the Lord, and by these efforts he hopes to kindle a love of divine Scripture [8]. The prominence of the term *ad fontes* never varies, but here we see the thought of Erasmus changing from sources in general toward a particular source that is enlightened by other sources. The Holy Scriptures are the most important source, the best of the sources.

From this development in the thought of Erasmus the Erasmian Reform emerges. In *Novum Testamentum Praefationes* the Holy Scripture is not only the highest source [9], but also the basis for

---

Theologiam, Holborn, 305.1, in which Erasmus states that piety is found in the sources: "At si quis magis cupit instructus esse ad pietatem quam ad disputationem, statim ac potissimum versetur in fontibus, versetur in his scriptoribus, qui proxime biberunt de fontibus."

8) *Enchiridion Militis Christiani*, Holborn, 135.23. "Atque ut intelligant calumniatores quidam, qui summam existimant religionem nihil bonarum litterarum scire, quod politiorem veterum litteraturam per adolescentiam sumus amplexi, quod utriusque linguae, Graecae pariter ac Latinae, mediocrem cognitionem non sine multis vigiliis nobis peperimus, non ad famam inanem aut puerilem animi voluptatem spectasse nos, sed multo ante fuisse praemeditatos, ut dominicum templum, quod nonulli inscitia barbarieque sua nimis dehonestarunt, exoticis opibus pro viribus exornaremus, quibus et generosa ingenia possent ad divinarum scripturarum amorem inflammari."

9) "Methodus", Holborn, 159.30. "Quod si quos deterret hic labor, illud quaeso secum cogitet, qui conveniat, ut theologus futurus sophisticas praeceptiunculas ediscat, ediscat qualiacunque in Aristotelem commentaria, ediscat Scoti conclusiones et argumenta, et idem operae gravetur dare libris divinis, ex quorum fontibus universa scatet theologia, quae modo vere sit theologia?" Cf. "Paraclesis", Holborn, 144.15. "Platonicus non est, qui Platonis libros non legerit, et theologus est, non modo Christianus, qui Christi litteras non legerit? Qui diligit, inquit, me, sermones meos servat, hanc ipse notam praescripsit." (Joan. 14.23)

Cf. ibid., 146.29. "Quid tandem hoc rei est? Litteras ab amiculo scriptas servamus, exosculamur, circumferimus, iterum atque iterum relegimus, et tot sunt milia Christianorum, qui cum alioqui docti sint, euangelicos et apostolicos libros ne legerint quidem unquam in omni vita. Mahumetaei sua tenent dogmata, Iudaei et hodie ab ipsis cunabulis suum ediscunt Mosen. Cur nos non idem praestamus Christo?"

10) Allen, 710.1 ff. To Cardinal Domenico Grimani of Rome. (Dedicatory epistle to "Paraphrasis ad Romanos") 13. Nov. 1517.
.60. "Adriai statuam aut Domitiani miraris thermas. Quin potius Petri Paulique sacrosanctas epistolas amplecteris?"

purifying the church [10]. As the ground of the Erasmian reform [11], Scripture is therefore the pristine source, rather than one among many sources [12]. We can see in this development that same insistence upon *ad fontes*, but now with a different application.

The expression *ad fontes* could easily be classified as a motto with Erasmus [13], but it is more than a mere motto because Erasmus saw in the sources an opportunity to rid contemporary Christianity and society of the excesses that he so despised: superstition and ignorance [14], and Scholastic theology [15].

Erasmus, therefore, not only took this byword of the Renaissance and, in a sense, Erasmusized it, but he also saw it as the means by which he could bring about his own personal reform — a reform that reached from the purification of the church and a true return to the teachings of Christ, to ridding society of the exorbitances

---

.71. "Si Ciceronis linguam miraris, de qua vix pronuncies plusne profuerit an obfuerit reipublicae, cur non magis delectat Paulina Facundia, cui salutis ac Religionis tuae summam debes?"

.108. (Speaking of Pope Leo X). "Id fiet, if Petri ac Pauli, quorum auspiciis praesidioque regnat, pectus vitamque pro viribus studeat exprimere. Atqui horum imaginem nusquam expressiorem magisque viuam liceat reperire quam in ipsorum literis."

11) "Methodus", Holborn, 162.15. "At simplices illae litterae totius orbis populos pauculis annis innovare potuerunt."
Cf. *Ratio ... ad veram Theologiam*, Holborn, 304.26. "Sed simplices illae litterae veritate, non argutia efficaces totius orbis populos pauculis annis innovare potuerunt."

12) *Ratio ... ad veram Theologiam*, Holborn, 204.11. "Maneat intactus ille scopus, sit illibatus unicus ille fons, servetur illa vere sacra ancora doctrinae euangelicae, ad quam in tanta rerum humanarum caligine confugere liceat."

13) Allen, 1144.18, "...; sed quod theologos ad fontes revocarim"; 1183.39. "...; ad divinae Scripturae fontes revocarim." 1225.219. "Loci communes quibus fere declamabam, faciunt adversus eos qui neglectis fontibus sacrorum voluminum, ..".

14) Ibid., 396.64. "Calceos sanctorum et sudariola mucco sordentia exosculamur, et eorundem libros, sanctissimas et efficacissimas diuorum reliquias, neglectos iacere patimur."

15) "Paraclesis", Holborn, 141.21. "Cur non hic pia curiositate singula cognoscimus, disquirimus, excutimus? Praesertim cum hoc sapientiae genus tam eximium, ut semel stultam reddiderit universam huius mundi sapientiam, ex paucis hisce libris velut e limpidissimis fontibus haurire liceat longe minore negotio quam ex tot voluminibus spinosis, ex tam immensis iisque inter se pugnantibus interpretum commentariis Aristotelicam doctrinam, ut ne addam quanto maiore cum fructu."

that were such a personal grievance to him. On the loftier side it was certainly a noble aim, especially if we consider that most of Erasmus' mature thoughts were formed long before Luther became known. But on the lower plane Erasmus used the sources unscrupulously to rid society of what he considered its most glaring negative aspects.

But the positive is wherein lies Erasmus' contribution; to deal only with the negative aspect is to miss the importance and the profoundness of his hermeneutical approach.

One of the most positive elements in the Erasmian reform is the Christological significance of Erasmus' approach. Since Erasmus saw the sources, in particular the Scriptures, as the means by which to bring about his reform, he also realized that there was more than just the dedicated study of the sources involved if this reform were to be carried out. This "more" is Christ [16]. The *philosophia Christi* is the purest source [17]. But only through studying the *fons* will this *philosophia Christi* bring about the desired reform. For it is in the sources that Christ lives, breathes, and speaks to us.

> "Moreover these sacred words give you the very image of Christ speaking, healing, dying, rising again, and make him so present, that were he before your very own eyes you would not more truly see him" [18].

Cf. ibid., 144.35. "Hoc philosophiae genus in affectibus situm verius quam in syllogismis vita magis est quam disputatio, afflatus potius quam eruditio, transformatio magis quam ratio."

Cf. "Methodus", Holborn, 162.2. "Praestat paulo minus esse sophistam quam minus sapere in euangeliis ac Paulinis litteris. Satius est ignorare quaedam Aristotelis dogmata quam nescire Christi decreta. Denique malim cum Hieronymo pius esse theologus quam cum Scoto invictus."

16) *Ratio ... ad veram Theologiam*, Holborn, 203.23. "Christus, ut purissimus ille fons omnis lucis et innocentiae, praecepit ea, quae caelum sapiant."

17) Ibid., 204.4. "Christianae philosophiae purissimum fontem."

18) "Paraclesis", Holborn, 149.8. "... at hae tibi sacrosanctae mentis illius vivam referunt imaginem ipsumque Christum loquentem, sanantem, morientem, resurgentem, denique totum ita praesentem reddunt, ut minus visurus sis, si coram oculis conspicias."

Cf. ibid., 146.23. "... in his litteris praecipue praestat, in quibus nobis etiamnum vivit, spirat, loquitur, paene dixerim efficacius, quam cum inter homines versaretur. Minus videbant, minus audiebant Iudaei, quam tu vides et audis in euangelicis litteris, ..."

14

The pedagogical aspects of the Erasmian reform are also rooted in the sources. Because the Scriptures are so important, people should be continually occupied with the Scriptures and instructed in them [19]. In fact, they are of such great importance that the most essential passages should be memorized by heart [20], not in summary form or recapitulations, but verbatim from the sources themselves [21].

The same is true for theology and the theologians. They are to learn Greek and Hebrew so that they will be able to theologize at the sources [22]. In fact, the aim of theology is to relate the knowledge of divine Scripture in matters of faith, piety, and the things of heaven [23]. Thinking as he did in this manner, it follows that Erasmus would want beginners in theology to start with the sources, first the gospels and then the books of the apostles [24]. This in itself was a radical departure from the established practices of his day, the consequences of such a program would be a certain degree of reform within the church.

Having established the importance of the term *ad fontes* in the development of Erasmus' thought as the means by which Erasmus wishes to carry out his reform, we can now analyze the term *fons*.

Although Scripture is the highest and prime source in the mature thought of Erasmus, nevertheless the sources remain plural for Erasmus. They include not only the Scriptures but also the classics,

---

19) "Methodus", Holborn, 159.18. "Atque hisce iam rebus instructus iugi meditatione versetur in divinis litteris, . . ."

20) Ibid., 159.23. "Nec fuerit inconsultum divinos libros ad verbum ediscere, praesertim novi testamenti, . . ."

21) Ibid., 158.6. "Admonendus, ut apposite condiscat citare divinae scripturae testimonia, non e summulis aut contiunculis aut collectaneis nescio quibus iam sescenties aliunde alio commixtis ac retusis, sed ex ipsis fontibus, . . ."

22) "Apologia", Holborn, 165.6. "Primum igitur etiam atque etiam adhortor omnes theologos, ut quibus per aetatem aut occupationes vacat, Graecas degustent litteras et item Hebraeas si liceat. In ipsis arcanae scripturae fontibus diligenter philosophentur, . . ."

23) *Ratio ... ad veram Theologiam*, Holborn, 193.18. "At praecipuus theologorum scopus est sapienter enarrare divinas litteras, de fide, non de frivolis quaestionibus rationem reddere, de pietate graviter atque efficaciter disserere, lacrimas excutere, ad caelestia inflammare animos."

24) Ibid., 193.24. "Illud mea sententia magis ad rem pertinuerit, ut tirunculo nostro dogmata tradantur in summam ac compendium redacta, idque potissimum ex euangelicis fontibus, mox apostolorum litteris, . . ."

for though the Scriptures have the highest place, Erasmus never forgets the importance of the ancients.

> "You will perhaps find in the books of Plato or of Seneca things which are not abhorrent to the teachings of Christ; you will find in the life of Socrates that which is consistent with the life of Christ. But you will find in Christ alone the congruity and harmony of all things" [25].

Christ was, for Erasmus, the highest manifestation of the concepts and ideals that are to be found in antiquity; the Scriptures, in a sense, sum up all the conceptions of which the classical writers in their best moments had glimpses.

The multiplicity of the sources is to remain with Erasmus throughout his entire life. Erasmus felt that Christian Humanism was the key to a better world. There was never any tension for Erasmus between the Christian religion and classical philosophy. Erasmus envisioned a classical world illuminated with the Christian faith. He wished to select the best of the classical ethic and teaching, and use them, since, seeing no conflict between them and Christianity, he felt that they were as perfect ethically as was to be found [26].

The study of the sources also meant for Erasmus that one should be cognizant of the general culture of antiquity, which includes interest in both education and nature [27]. It is worth noting that

---

25) Ibid., 210.33. "Reperies fortassis in Platonis aut Senecae libris, quae non abhorrent a decretis Christi; reperies in vita Socratis, quae utcumque cum Christi vita consentiant. At circulum hunc et omnium rerum inter se congruentium harmoniam in solo Christo reperies."
This idea is a continuation of the Apologists in the second century, and a foreshadowing of *Aufklärung* thought in the eighteenth century.

26) *Colloquia Familiarae,* "Convivium Religiosum", LB i, 672 ff. (see particularly 683 d). "Proinde mihi nihil unquam legisse videor apud Ethnicos, quod aptius quadret in hominem vere Christianum, quam quod Socrates paulo post bibiturus cicutam, . . ."
Cf. Allen, 1013.44. Preface to Cicero's "De Officiis". "At in praeceptis viuendi quanta aequitas, quanta sanctimonia, quanta synceritas, quanta veritas, quam omnia consentanea naturae, quam nihil fucatum aut somnolentum."

27) *Ratio . . . ad veram Theologiam,* Holborn, 184.23. "Porro si rara quaedam felicitas et alba quod dici solet indoles insignem theologum polliceri videbitur, haud mihi displicet, quod in libris de doctrina Christiana placuit Augustino, ut cautim ac moderate degustatis elegantioribus disciplinis per aetatem instituatur ac praeparetur, nempe dialectica, rhetorica, arithmetica, musica, cum primis autem rerum naturalium cognitione, velut siderum, animantium, arborum, gemmarum, ad haec locorum, praesertim eorum, quos divinae litterae commemorant."

Erasmus points them out as having a Biblical basis, giving Biblical sanctity to his cultural reform, and indirectly elevating the classical writings (observe that he uses the highly revered Augustine for this) to a position of authoriy. Naturally they were already authoritative to a certain degree to anyone who had a Renaissance bent, but here Erasmus is trying to impress the Scholastic theologians and monks with their importance.

Because Erasmus is so deeply devoted to the Renaissance, his thoughts and writings are continually changing from the classical sources to the Christian sources. To speak of one without the other is impossible for him. He could no more envision a Christian world without classicism than he could a classical world without Christianity. But the underlying principle remains Christian, and antiquity remains the form in which he wishes to put his Christian ideal to work.

Ad fontes also represents an exegetical method. In Erasmus' day the existing copies of the classics were so full of errors that it was difficult for one to know whether or not he was reading what the original author had said or what had come into the text through errors of copyists or inadvertent additions of notes on the part of the copyist. Since all copy had been done by hand up until the advent of the printing press in the fifteenth century, errors were bound to occur, either unintentionally through mistakes, or because some of the copyists knew neither the Greek nor the Latin that they were copying, therefore making a correct copy all but impossible. Erasmus not only had a firm conviction that one must go to the sources, but he must also go to the correct sources.

> "I am not unaware of the difficulty of the task, I might say, one worthy of Apollo, in restoring the works of Jerome which partly from lack of education are corrupted, and partly from an insufficient knowledge of Greek literature and antiquities have become undecipherable, blotted out, mutilated, erroneous and full of fiction" [28].

Cf. "Methodus", Holborn, 153.20. "Porro si rara quaedam ingenii felicitas et alba quod dici solet indoles insignem theologum polliceri videbitur, haud mihi displicet, quod placuit et Augustino, ut moderate degustatis elegantioribus disciplinis instruatur ac praeparetur, nempe dialectica, rhetorica, arithmetica, musica, astrologia, cum primis autem rerum naturalium cognitione velut animantium, arborum, gemmarum, ad haec locorum, praesertim illorum, quos divinae litterae commemorant."

28) Allen, 149.56. "Praeterea molior arduum quoddam et, vt ita dicam, Phaethonteum facinus, vt Hieronymianos libros partim ab iis semidoctis de-

Therefore *ad fontes* must concern itself with text criticism, both literary and philological. In trying to apply his principle of *ad fontes*, Erasmus spent a great deal of his life putting out new and, to the best of his ability, textually correct editions of the sources — Scripture, classics, both Latin and Greek, and the Church Fathers. He pictured himself as a lexigrapher of the ancient texts. It was a necessity, as he saw it, to restore these texts and re-establish them with precision. He took his principle of textual correctness even so far as to say that his beloved Jerome had erred in his translation [29]. The sources themselves were not sufficient unless they were textually corrected and pure. If one is to study the sources, then one must have a text available that allows him to come to grips with the technique, figures of speech, satire, irony, grammar, play on words, meaning, etc., of the author. In Erasmus' principles of correct textual restoration and textual study of the sources we see his exegetical technique taking shape. There is a form of text criticism that includes both a literary and a philological side.

The restoration of the text also accentuates the necessity of a comprehensive knowledge of the original languages. Erasmus, in his *Ratio seu Methodus compendio perveniendi ad veram Theologiam*, stresses the importance of the three theological languages, Greek, Latin, and Hebrew [30], and illustrates how there can be no true theological understanding without a thorough apprehension of these languages [31].

---

prauatos, partim ob rerum antiquarum et Graecae literaturae inscitiam aut obliteratos aut truncos aut mutilos aut certe mendosos et portentis plenos, ..."

29) "Methodus", Holborn, 152.1. "Neque enim audiendos arbitror istos quosdam, qui cum in sophisticis tricis usque ad decrepitam aetatem computrescant, dicere solent: 'Mihi satis est interpretatio Hieronymi.' Sic enim potissimum respondent ii, qui ne Latine quidem scire curant, ut his etiam frustra verterit Hieronymus."

30) *Ratio*, Holborn, 181.15. "Iam quod ad eas attinet litteras, quarum adminiculo commodius ad haec pertingimus, citra controversiam prima cura debetur perdiscendis tribus linguis, Latinae, Graecae et Hebraicae, quod constet omnem scripturam mysticam hisce proditam esse."
Cf. also the same words in "Methodus", Holborn, 151.25.

31) Ibid., 266.5. "Sunt autem tropi, qui non pertineant ad grammaticos aut rhetores, sed pertinent ad idioma sermonis, quod si ignoretur, frequenter aut fallit aut moratur lectorem. Ac Graeca quidem lingua complures habet cum Latina communes, quosdam habet sibi peculiares. Ceterum Hebraea plurimas habet loquendi formas ab utraque dissonantes. Commune est nobis cum Graecis, quod dicimus benefacere eum, qui bene, meretur de quopiam;

Erasmus relies entirely upon philology to make his point here. First he shows the similarities between Greek and Latin, and how Greek can be translated directly into Latin and still maintain its true meaning (ἔχω χάριν and *habeo gratiam*). Then he points out that without a thorough knowledge of both Greek and Latin, the differences can lead to a theological misunderstanding (ἔλαθεν ξενίσας ἀγγέλους, *qui insciens accepit angelos hospitio; at non item Latine: latuit accipiens angelos*). Theology, for Erasmus, must be cognizant of philology in order to perform its task. This illustration points out the fact that philological exegesis must be incorporated into theological studies, philology necessarily presupposing an exact knowledge of the Biblical languages.

Though Erasmus always stressed the necessity of learning all three of the Biblical languages, Greek was the most important[32]. There can be no doubt as to the primary reason that the learning of Greek was so important to Erasmus. To Antony, Abbot of Saint Bertin, he writes:

"Latin erudition, however opulent, is crippled and imperfect without Greek. We have in Latin at best some small streams and torpid pools, while Greek has the purest springs and rivers flowing with gold. I see it as madness to touch with the littlest finger that principal part of theology, which treats of divine mysteries, without being instructed in Greek, when those who have translated the sacred books have in their scrupulous interpretation so rendered the Greek phrases that even the primary meaning that our theologians call 'literal' cannot be understood by those who do not know Greek"[33].

---

at non item commune, quod illi dicunt εὐπαθεῖν, id est bene pati, pro eo quod est beneficio affici. Commune est cum illis, quod pro ἔχω χάριν dicimus: habeo gratiam. Non est commune, quod illi pro eodem dicunt: οἶδα χάριν, id est: novi gratiam aut μεμνήσομαι χάριν id est: meminero gratiam, pro eo, quod Latine diceretur: referam gratiam. Emendate dicitur Graecis: ἔλαθεν ξενίσας ἀγγέλους, qui insciens accepit angelos hospitio; at non item Latine: latuit accipiens angelos." (Heb. 13.2).

32) "Apologia", Holborn, 169.36. "Mihi plurimis argumentis vehementer probabile est universum instrumentum novum Graece scriptum fuisse, non Latine."

33) Allen, 149.17. "... Latinam eruditionem, quamuis impendiosam, citra Graecismum mancam esse ac dimidiatam. Apud nos enim riuuli vix quidam sunt et lacunulae lutulentae; apud illos fontes purissimi et flumina aurum voluentiae. Video dementiam esse extremam, theologiae partem quae de mysteriis est praecipua digitulo attingere, nisi quis Graecanica etiam sit instructus supellectile, cum ii qui diuinos vertere libros, religione transferendi ita Graecas

This knowledge of linguistics is to be used for text criticism to supplement theological erudition.

The exegetical approach found in *ad fontes* is also found in Erasmus' extensive use of the term *bonae litterae*. *Bonae litterae* not only means good literature, but it also encompasses the whole of good learning of which good literature; antique literature, is the means to his good learning. The term is best understood as embracing all of antiquity, its culture and literature, its learning and life. To translate the term literally is to do harm to the meaning that Erasmus applies to it.

To illustrate the broad meaning of *bonae litterae*, and what it includes in literature, listen to Erasmus as he speaks to his friend, Lord Montjoy, in the dedicatory epistle of his *Adagiorum Chilades*, printed in Venice in 1508:

> "I had some intention of appending a collection of distinguished metaphores, elegant sayings, witty allusions, and poetical allegories ... and add with special care the allegories of sacred literature from the ancient theologians" [34].

Implicit in this paragraph is the textual and philological analysis found in *ad fontes*.

As *bonae litterae* in its literary meaning includes all of classical literature, the Church Fathers, and the Scriptures, in its broader meaning it also embraces the entirety of good learning from the classical and Christian world.

> "There are some here who are deeply hostile toward me because I am credited with having introduced languages and secular literature into their branch of studies ... I have always favored evangelical learning and the glory of Christ, and, so far, I have favored secular learning that it might serve Christ" [35].

---

reddant figuras, vt ne primarius quidem ille, quem nostrates theologi literalem nominant, sensus percipiatur ab iis que Graece nesciunt."
Cf. ibid., 129.66. "Verum Graece te scire, mi Batte, percupio, tum quod sine litteras Latinas mancas esse video, ..."

34) Ibid., 211.20. "..., adiungere metaphoras insignes, scite dicta, sententias eximias, allusiones venustiores, allegorias poeticas, ... accuratius autem arcanarum literarum allegorias ex veteribus illis theologis statueram annectere ..."

35) Ibid., 1219.10. "Sunt hic aliquot mihi plusquam capitaliter infensi, quod linguas ac bonas literas credar in ipsorum regnum inuexisse."
Ibid., .47. "Euangelicae doctrinae Christi que gloriae semper faudi, bonis literis hactenus faudi, vt seruirent gloriae Christi."

Since Erasmus includes *sacres* and *saeculares* writings in this broad concept of *bonae litterae* and since he also includes *liberalia studia* [36] or *bona studia* in his definition, he is opening the door to a synthesis between culture and Christianity. Moreover, *bonae litterae* bridges the gap between natural revelation and divine revelation and influences the church toward an acceptance of secular literature.

That *bonae litterae* not only contains all of the aforementioned matter, but also encompasses the science of theology, is evident in this letter to John Colet:

> "In our day, those who apply themselves to the study of theology, the principal part of all literature, through their dullness and lack of sense, are scarcely fitted for literature at all . . ." [37].

In his "Apologia" in *Novum Testamentum Praefationes* Erasmus says that *bonae litterae* is in part indebted to Laurentius Valla, that controversial figure of the Italian Renaissance of the fifteenth century [38]. To use the name of Valla in such a way, especially in an introduction to the New Testament, is certainly to give the phrase *bonae litterae* a broad meaning, for Valla was a typical example of the baser side of the Italian movement. There can be no doubt as to the broadness of *bonae litterae* for Erasmus when we consider statements like the above.

Not only is *bonae litterae* all encompassing in its broadness of meaning, but it is also the means by which we understand the Gospel. It is through this learning that we come to true knowledge and understanding [39]. Even though men have attributed to Erasmus a great importance to the motivation of reason in his thought, learning is far more important to him than reason. To understand theology requires learning; to understand the Scriptures requires

---

36) Ibid., 993.62. "Illud mihi molestum est, quod his sycophantiis inficiuntur liberalia studia."

37) Ibid., 108.48. "... quod nostra tempestate fere ad theologiae studium sese applicant, litterarum omnium principem, qui propter ingenium pingue parumque sanum vix vllis sunt litteris idonei."

38) "Apologia", Holborn, 174.1. "Laurentium Vallam, cui non hac tantum in parte debent bonae litterae."

39) *Enchiridion,* Holborn, 67.16. "Sed cum Paulo (1 Cor. 12.31) viam demonstro excellentiorem. Ad hanc regulam si studia et actus omnes tuos excusseris neque usquam constiteris in mediis, donec perveneris usque ad Christum."

study. Many of his compositions are written as aids to better education and learning [40].

Bonae litterae is not only the means by which one understands, but it is also the means by which this understanding is carried into the practical realm [41]. *Bonae litterae* promotes a better ethic and culture. Because we understand what superstition is and the underlying principles behind it, we are able to do away with it. The same is true of ignorance, vulgarity, wars, and all that is coarse and common. Here *bonae litterae* is a means to understanding and a concept to rid the world of its non-understanding. In writing to John Colet, Erasmus sums up this aspect of *bonae litterae:*

> "Truly your England is delightful to me for many reasons, but most of all it abounds in what pleases me more than anything else, I mean in men most proficient in *bonae litterae,* you being the principal figure" [42].

No matter how much confidence Erasmus put in *bonae litterae* as the key to understanding and no matter how important he felt its impact on culture should be, Erasmus never forgot the fact that if *bonae litterae* ever lost sight of the Gospel and failed to recognize the simplicities of the Gospel, then it was deceiving itself and was therefore no longer good learning. *Bonae litterae* must necessarily be closely connected to the Gospel and Christ in order to fulfill its true meaning. "The greatest teacher is he who teaches Christ" [43]. One cannot help but wonder if Erasmus would not have liked this statement to be a self-portrait.

This practical realm of *bonae litterae* is also a means by which Erasmus wished to carry out his reform. It is here that the terms

---

40) Even some of Erasmus' major works are study guides. See *Ratio ... ad veram Theologiam*, Holborn, 177.3 ff where Erasmus discusses the importance of true theological study. Also Louis Bouyer, *Autour D'Erasme* (Paris, 1955), in his section, "La Ratio Verae Theologiae", p. 141: Quel est exactement le propos de la Ratio? ... Comme beaucoup d'ouvrages d'Erasme, c'est un manuel d'étudiant. Nous l'intitulerions aujourd'hui: Introduction aux études théologiques."

41) Huizinga, p. 150. "Und das Mittel zu all dem war echte Bildung, bonae litterae."

42) Allen, 107.50. "Anglia vero tua mihi quum multis nominibus tum hoc praecipue nmine iucundissima est, quod iis rebus abundans, praeter quas nihil mihi solet esse iucundum, hominibus bonarum literarum scientissimis, inter quos, nomine reclamante, facile te principem numero."

43) "Methodus", Holborn, 162.26, and *Ratio*, Holborn, 305.10. "Abunde magnus doctor est, qui pure docet Christum."

ad fontes and *bonae litterae* take on a synonymous meaning, and Erasmus can use either one to state his reform. Since the Erasmian reform has already been covered under the term *ad fontes*, it suffices here to point out the synonymous meaning in which Erasmus uses these two terms.

The most important aspect of *bonae litterae* in carrying out the Erasmian reform is the restoration of theology, for Erasmus saw in *bonae litterae* an opportunity to restore theology to the place he felt it should have and to restore to theology the type of learning it should entail. To Louis Ber he writes: "I have developed language and cultured literature for the good of theology" [44]. Cultured or classical literature was to be an uplifting force to the theology of that day, while the languages were to lead to a deeper philological knowledge of the sources.

Erasmus saw, perhaps naively, in *bonae litterae*, a cure-all for everything that he disliked, and as the means of returning to the pureness and simplicity that he felt the classical world, Christianized, of course, offered. *Bonae litterae* was to be the means to reform all that he considered vulgar and intellectually stifling. But he realized early that it was a difficult task, for the monks and the leaders of theology were not to be changed easily.

> "It is truly no secret to me that I have pursued a kind of study which some think strange, others endless, others unprofitable, others even impious; certainly to those who are men of letters" [45].

In the scholastic system, Erasmus saw a chief threat to the good learning that he so desired. While he himself was anything but moderate in the things of which he approved, yet he would plead for moderation when studying the prevalent courses in the schools of his day [46]. Since Erasmus did not have the power to eliminate this form and method of learning, he implies that it should not be taken too seriously.

---

44) Allen, 2136.185. "Prouixi linguas ac politiores litteras magno rei theologicae bono."

45) Ibid., 161.29. "Neque vero me clam est, hoc quod sum sequutus studiorum genus aliis alienum, aliis infinitum, aliis infrugiferum, aliis etiam parum pium videri; nempe vulgo omnium qui nunc literas profitentur."

46) *Ratio ... ad veram Theologiam*, Holborn, 191.31. "Neque vero haec eo dixerim, quod damnem ea studia, quae nunc fere videmus in publicis scholis solemnia, modo sobrie casteque tractentur neque sola tamen."

Bonae litterae as a means to the Erasmian reform has both its positive and negative side. The positive is always aimed at a real reform of theology and a return to Christ and the teachings of the Gospels. The negative side is aimed at a change in culture, a move from the darkness of the Middle Ages toward the light of antiquity, and it is under this negative tabulation that Erasmus places everything that he personally dislikes. The positive approach has value since in it we find constructive ideas of reforming the church of his day, while the negative side has value in that here we find insights into the personality of Erasmus.

There can be no doubt of the importance of this term *bonae litterae* for Erasmus, for time and time again he uses it to express his desire for its triumph. To Pope Leo X, upon his election to the papacy, Erasmus writes that with Leo as Pope, true religion and *bonae litterae* will flourish [47]. When commenting on his edition of the New Testament he says, "In our humble position we are making all the efforts we can to help the cause of literature" [48]. The definite connection between Christianity and *bonae litterae* in Erasmus' thought is apparent when we consider statements like these.

Just as Erasmus never missed an opportunity of attacking the opponents of *bonae litterae*, he could never forego the chance, if it presented itself, to promote this conception that was so important to him. In the introduction to his poem, "Prosopopeia Britanniae", dedicated to Duke Henry, who was later to become Henry VIII, we find Erasmus concluding, "Farewell, and may *bonae litterae* be illustrated by your splendor, protected by your authority, and supported by your liberality" [49].

Because of his acquaintance with the leading personalities of his age and his never-ending quest for *bonae litterae*, the influence of Erasmus in promoting *bonae litterae* was tremendous. One needs only to read very little by or about Erasmus to become impressed

---

47) Allen, 335.331. "Et pulchre videtur conuenire vt omnes *bonae litterae*, quae pacis alumnae sunt, per eum Pontificem reflorescant, per quem ocium et pax studiorum altrix orbi terrarum parta est; et pulchre quadrauerit vt primus Christianae religionis Doctor eiusdem religionis Antistiti summo dedicetur, et optimus omnium theologus omnium optimi Pontificis titulo commendetur."

48) Ibid., 407.7. "Nos humiles quod licet molimur et rei litterariae succurrimus pro virili."

49) Ibid., 104.66. "Bene vale, et bonas litteras splendore tuo illustra, auctoritate tuere, liberalitate foue."

by the influence he was able to exert on his times in the cause of this new learning.

But Erasmus was also a product of this new learning and very much under the influence of it. This is shown clearly throughout his works and particularly in a letter to Andraes Ammonias, perhaps the most faithful friend he ever had. To Ammonias Erasmus does not hesitate to use the expression, *afflatus a deo quopiam* (influenced by some god) [50]. This phrase, actually pagan in origin and pagan sounding, shows the influence of the Renaissance upon Erasmus, and demonstrates his desire to imitate the classical learning. Erasmus uses expressions of this nature not as a sign of conviction, but only to impress others with his culture and learning. After all, *bonae litterae* meant a great deal to Erasmus, and he was no doubt pleased when given the opportunity to show that he was one of the learned.

Erasmus was never able to distinguish the true difference between a Christian world and a classical world that was Christianized. His conception of *bonae litterae* included much more than it should have, and the idea that there was only a qualitative dissimilarity between Christianity and Classicism was to cause him a great deal of grief. The Reformers were never able to equate these two mutually exclusive concepts and therefore Erasmus felt that their thrust sometimes endangered the cause of *bonae litterae*, when in actuality they had little interest in the cause *per se*. But the very fact that the Reformers, especially Luther, did not equate Christianity and Classicism made Erasmus feel that all his concepts were being attacked. To George Spalatin Erasmus wrote:

> "I would prefer Luther to refrain from these contentions for a little while, and to expound the Gospel simply, without admixture of personal feelings: perhaps his undertaking would succeed better. Now he is exposing even *bonae litterae* to an ill will which is ruinous to us and unprofitable to himself" [51].

---

50) Ibid., 273.14. "Ad Hieronymum emendandum et scholiis illustrandum ita mihi feruet animus vt afflatus a deo quopiam mihi videar."

51) Ibid., 1119.34. July 6, 1520. "Optarim Lutherum ab istis contentionibus aliquantisper conquiescere, ac rem Euangelicam tractare pure, non admixtis affectibus: fortasse res aliquanto melius successerit. Nunc et bonas literas degrauat inuidia nobis exitiabili, ipsi infrugifera."
Cf. ibid., 1185.19. "Lutherus maxima inuidia grauet et nos et bona studia."
Of course one of the basic problems between Erasmus and Luther lay in their

That Erasmus put too much emphasis on the principle of *bonae litterae* cannot be debated, and because of this he saw every attack upon it as a personal attack upon himself [52]. He grossly misinterpreted the situation and the times when he said that the origin of the persecution of Luther was hatred of *bonae litterae* and love of tyranny [53]. The idealist was never quite able to come to grips with the complicated phenomena that lay behind the Reformation and the struggle that ensued.

Erasmus' use of the term *ad fontes* represents, among other things, an exegetical method. It is this exegetical method that sets him apart from the traditional hermeneutic of his times. For in *ad fontes* Erasmus sees text criticism playing an important part, and text criticism necessarily demands an exact knowledge of the Biblical languages. Moreover, text criticism has for Erasmus both a literary and a philological aspect. The method in which Erasmus uses *ad fontes* is thus his means of getting to the original and genuine meaning of the text.

The fact that Erasmus used the sources does not separate him from the Middle Age theorists of interpretation, for they too used the sources. But it is the method that Erasmus sets forth that differs from the typical Middle Age hermeneutic.

---

differences of personality, so when Luther "aired his personal feelings", Erasmus felt he did it in a *via barbara*, thereby hurting the cause of *bonae litterae*.

52) Ibid., 1418.18. To Clement VII. "Theologorum ac monachorum odiis, qui me ob inuectas apud nos et euectas linguas ac bonas literas peius oderunt quam Lutherum."
Ibid., 1195.19. "Sed illud fuit commentum quorundam monachorum, quibus non aliter charus sum quam bonae literae, vt me volentem nolentem involuerent Lutherano negocio."
Ibid., 1225.182. "Non ignorabam quam pertinacibus odiis me insectarentur quidem apud nostros, odio bonarum literarum."
Ibid., 1432.64. "In Brebantia scis quot annis digladiatus sim cum theologis, qui peius oderunt bonas literas quam Lutherum."
Ibid., 1434.36. "Scis quanta mihi fuerit digladiato cum theologis quibusdam ob bonas literas ante Lutheri exortum."

53) "Axiomata Erasmi pro Causa Martini Lutheri", Ferguson, p. 336.3. "Fons rei malus est: odium bonarum litterarum et affectatio tyrannidis."
Cf. Allen, 1141.25. "Ex odio bonarum literarum et stoliditate monachorum primum orta est haec tragoedia."
Cf. ibid., 1167.72. "Hic igitur est fons ac seminarium huius totius tragoediae, immedicabile odium linguarum ac bonarum literarum."

The Scholastics' emphasis lay primarily in their method. They sought a synthesis of knowledge, and they wished to classify this knowledge in a rationalistic way. They used the highly technical Latin of the Middle Ages, and took great delight in the different shades of meaning that it was capable of bringing out. The method was, in a sense, an exercise in classifying and distinguishing between different thoughts in what came to be a set form: *Quaestio...* *Utrum ... Videtur quod ... Sed Contra est ... Responsio.* The problem itself was the important thing to be resolved and the means was reason in the context of faith, but always in the setting of the standard method.

Erasmus rejected the Scholastic theology along with its form and style [54]. He considered Scotus and his type useful for study but useless for speech [55]. He went even further in his *Ratio verae theologiae* when he stated that the *scholastica dogmata* are not articles of faith [56]. But above all Erasmus felt that the Scholastic theology was irrelevant and had little to say to mankind concerning Christ. "I see the simple multitude longing after food for their soul, desiring to learn how they can return to their homes better people, and then the lecturer (theologaster) ... ventilates some frigid and perplexing question from Scotus or Occam" [57]. In the *Enchiridion* he wrote that "Scotus seems to have given these men such great confidence that, without ever having read the Sacred Writings, they still think themselves to be unlimited theologians" [58].

---

54) Allen, 1747.96. "Tertia causa est huic similis, quod in scriptis meis alicubi dissentiam a Scoto, Thoma, Lyrano, Hugone; deinde quod indico subinde quibus in rebus sita sit vera religio."

55) LB v, 877 d, *Enchiridion* II. "Scotus, et hujus similes ad rerum cognitionem utiles sunt, ad dicendum inutiles."

56) Holborn, 205.15. "Neque secus sentiendum de dogmatis scholasticis, habeant illa sane pondus suum in palaestris disputationum, adhibeantur ut humana placita, ut themata argumentaque conflictationum, non ut articuli fidei, praesertim cum in his nec ipsae inter se scholae consentiant nec iisdem interim eadem perpetuo placeant."

57) Ibid., 301.14. "Video simplicem multitudinem hiantem et avidam pendere ab ore contionantis, exspectare pabulum animi sui cupidam discendi, quo melior domum redeat, et ibi mihi theologiaster quispiam fere ἱεροπρεπεῖ σχήματι venerandus e Scoto aut Occam quaestionem aliquam frigidam ac perplexam ventilat ostentans, ..."

58) Ibid., 34.3. "... tantumque illis fiduciam Scotus faciebat, ut ne lectis quidem unquam sacris litteris se tamen absolutos theologos putarent."

At the same time Erasmus' definition of faith differs intrinsically from the Scholastic position of a relationship between knowledge and belief. Peter Lombard [59], following Augustine, defines three different types of belief: 1. *Credere Deo*, 2. *Credere Deum*, 3. *Credere in Deum*. The first means to believe that the things God says are true, the second means to believe in the existence of God, and the third means to love Him by faith, which is belief in the full sense of the word. Anselm of Canterbury tied faith to reason when he said, *"Credo ut intelligam"* [60]. The starting point of Anselm is that we must begin with faith in order to arrive at understanding. As time went on there developed a separation of faith and reason, so that Duns Scotus could speak of two different types of faith: an acquired faith (*fides acquisita*; faith which man can acquire for himself), which acknowledges the possibility of explaining faith in a natural way, and an infused faith (*fides infusa*; faith which is created by God), which is necessary to recognize the authority of Scripture and the saints [61]. Faith for the Scholastics was a phenomenon that must be carefully explained and qualified, while for Erasmus it is simply *fidicuciam, collocare in Deo* [62].

The Middle Age hermeneutic was the by-product of the Scholastic method and this method was primarily interested in a logical, orderly, and exhaustive approach to Scripture. The device that these exegetes used to expound their method was the *glossa*. Normally there were two glosses, an interlinear and a marginal one. The interlinear gloss was a paraphrase of the text, stressing meanings

Johannes Duns Scotus had the title "Doctor subtilis" and Erasmus is continually satirizing this term "subtilis" in his writings. He finds great sport in calling all Scholastics "Scotists" and in his satirical use of the honored title "Magistri nostri".

59) *Sent.* III, dist. 23, cat. 4.

60) *Proslogium*, chapter 1.

61) *Sent.* III, d. 23, q. 1,4 ff; 6,14. "De primo certum est, quod in nobis est fides reuelatorum credibilium acquisita ... Credo igitur fide acquisita Euangelio, quia Ecclesia tenet scriptores veraces, quod ego audiens acquiro mihi habitum credendi dictis illorum."
"Secundo de fide infusa, quomodo sit ponenda in nobis, et hoc non est ita certum, an sit, vel quomodo sit ponenda in nobis; ... Ad quaestionem tamen dico, quod oportet ponere fidem infusam propter auctoritatem scripturae, et sanctorum ..."

62) Holborn, 237.18. "Fides praestat, ut nobis diffisi fiduciam omnem collocemus in deo."
Cf. LB v, 777, 798, 1079, 1147, 1166.

of important words and the logical connection between them. The marginal gloss consisted of brief interpretations of the text excerpted from the recognized authorities. These glosses based the interpretation of the text on the theological exposition of individual words and terms, making it easy to lose sight of the overall thrust of the passage.

Aside from the gloss, there was the *scholia*. This was much the same, but it was primarily used for practical exegesis or extensive interpretation of certain important passages, or to refute the arguments of opponents [63].

Thomas Aquinas has even further appendages — distinctions in the text, divisions of these distinctions, followed by questions and articulations on the questions. This method represents an exhaustive study, but it is primarily based on an intellectual accumulation rather than a philological critical interest in the text.

In his *Commentary to Matthew* (chapter 9.1 ff.), Aquinas plainly illustrates this method of interpretation when he not only lists the miracles but also divides them into groups and subgroups and under categories such as *finus*, *modus*, and *efficientia* [64]. It is a comprehensive study, not based on the sources themselves, but on a collection and classification of material.

Nicholas of Lyra advocates four rules for the proper understanding of the Scriptures. The first deals with Jesus Christ and his Church. The second, with the true body of Christ. The third rule deals with the spirit and the letter (in one and the same word there is to be found an historical and a mystical meaning). The fourth, with the species and the genus, or with the part of the whole; with the transition from one to the other and conversely [65].

Following Lyra's writings the discussion centered upon the meaning of the *sensus litteralis*, if the literal sense should be based on the *sensus litteralis historicus* (the intended meaning of the writer) or on the *sensus litteralis propheticus* (the meaning that the Holy Spirit intended).

---

63) Unlike Erasmus, who used neither *glossa* nor *scholia*, but rather annotations and paraphrases.

64) *Opera,* Thomas Aquinas, vol. 10, Parma 1861, pp. 88a, 89b.

65) *Postillae perpetuae in Vetus et Novum Testamentum,* prologue ii. "Quarta regula est de specie et sive de parte a toto cum de uno transit ad aliud et e converso."

As if all these technicalities of the interpretation were not enough, the Middle Ages had also developed the four-fold sense of interpretation. Origen had developed a three-fold method in interpreting Scripture based on a trichotomy: body, soul, and spirit. The body, *soma*, concerned itself with the moral or tropological sense; the soul, *psyche*, with the allegorical sense; and the spirit, *pneuma*, concerned itself with the anagogical meaning of the Scriptures. In the fifth century John Cassianus had expanded this three-fold sense of interpretation into a four-fold sense. This was later to be expanded into a formula that every student of theology in the Middle Age was forced to memorize:

"Littera gesta doctet, quid credas allegoria,
Moralis quid agas, sed quid speres anagoge."

However, Thomas Aquinas had stated in his *Summa Theologia* that nothing can be bound together under the spiritual sense as necessary for the faith that Scripture does not somewhere plainly hand down through its literal meaning [66].

As this brief historical review illustrates, the Middle Ages' theology had never lost contact with Scriptures, but the *expositio textus* had become so interwoven with the complicated Scholastic method that it was no longer based on Scriptures as a starting point. The *quaestiones* became the primary concern of theology just as the use of the four-fold sense of interpretation was superimposed on exegesis. The *lingua Biblica* became expressed in Scholastic terminology.

Erasmus shows, especially in his earlier writings, that he was very much under the influence of this four-fold sense of interpretation, particularly with the allegorical sense. In the *Enchiridion Militis Christiani* he wrote,

"From the interpreters of Holy Scripture choose those who depart as far as possible from the literal sense. After Paul the first are Origen, Ambrose, Jerome, and Augustine. For I see the modern theologians adhering to the letter rather than giving their attention to the mysteries, as if Paul had not spoken truly that our law is spiritual" [67].

66) *Summa Theologia*, I, q. 1, a. 10. "Nihil sub spirituali sensu continetur fide necessarium quod Scriptura per literalem sensum alicubi manifeste non tradet." The *sensus litteralis* or *historicus* was the real basis of interpretation for the Middle Ages since they felt it was inadmissible to render a passage in the *sensus spiritualis* that was clearly shown somewhere in Scripture in a literal or historical meaning.

However, Erasmus was to take a radical departure from his earlier days in the *Ecclesiastes* (1535), which is his writing on homiletics, when he wrote that the preacher should go to the sources themselves to deduce from that which precedes and from that which follows, the natural sense of the Scriptures [68].

Erasmus offers another sharp contrast to Scholastic interpretation of Scripture when he states in the dedicatory epistle to his paraphrases on Romans that his purpose in these paraphrases is to help the reader to arrive at the original and genuine meaning of the text. This is in direct opposition to the traditional method of elaborating on every detail. Erasmus shows that this clarification of the text means that it is the paraphraser's job to throw light on difficult passages, to explain where explanations are needed, and in general to do anything that can help the reader to better understand. The aim is pedagogical, but the method is based on a form of text criticism, which is primarily rooted in philology. "To close the gulfs, to soften abrupt transitions, and to smooth out confused sentences" [69] has all the characteristics of philology. Since there is an entire chapter devoted to the philology of Erasmus, we can briefly summarize here by stating that this philological method of text criticism that is rooted in the text itself differs radically from the hermeneutical approach of the Middle Ages.

Luther, unlike Erasmus, was not so interested in breaking with the Scholastic method of exegesis [70]. Erasmus hated the Scholastic method because it stood in direct opposition to his humanistic concepts and ideals, but Luther developed his exegetical method and theological understanding through a thorough knowledge and use of all the previous interpreters, whether ancient, Scholastic, or of his own time. Furthermore, Luther had an exceptional knowl-

---

67) *Enchiridion*, Holborn, 33.31. "Ex interpretibus divinae scripturae eos potissimum delige, qui a littera quammaxime recedunt. Cuiusmodi sunt in primis post Paulum Origenes, Ambrosius, Hieronymus, Augustinus. Video enim neotericos theologos litterae nimium libenter inhaerere et captiosis quibusdam argutiis magis quam eruendis mysteriis operam dare, quasi vero non vere dixerit Paulus legem nostram spiritualem esse."

68) LB v, 1026. "... ipsos adeat fontes, atque ex, iis quae praecedunt, quaeque sequuntur, germanum Scripturae sensum rimetur."

69) Allen, 710.26. "Quid sit hiantia committere, abrupta mollire, confusa digerere, inuoluta euoluere, nodosa explicare, obscuris lucem addere, ..."

70) Luther was trained in the Scholastic *Schule* and his textbooks were those of the Scholastics.

edge of the Scholastic theology and exegesis. He had even taught a course on the *Quatuor libri sententiarum* of Peter Lombard while at the University of Erfurt in 1509 and 1510[71]. It is also evident from his early exegetical work that Luther was well acquainted with both the method and theology of such Scholastics as Duns Scotus, and especially the nominalists, William of Occam, Pierre d'Ailly, and Gabriel Biel. These early lectures on the epistles of Paul also point out that Luther knew well Nicholas of Lyra, not to mention his favorites, Augustine and Bernard of Clairvaux and ancients like Jerome and Ambrose, as well as the latest available exegetical helps of his day such as the works of Lefèvre, Erasmus, and Reuchlin's Hebrew lexicon.

But before we illustrate Luther's use of the Scholastics' method and their exegesis, it is only fair to Luther to quote his statement pointing out the radical division of thought between himself and the Scholastics:

> "As for me, I know and confess that I learned nothing from Scholastic theology but ignorance of sin, righteousness, baptism, and of the entire Christian life. I certainly did not learn from them what the power of God is, and the work of God, the grace of God, and the righteousness of God, and what faith, hope and love are ... Indeed I lost Christ there, but now I have found him again in Paul"[72].

In Luther's *Römerbriefvorlesung*, 1515—1516, *Galaterbriefvorlesung*, 1516—1517, and *Hebräerbriefvorlesung*, 1517—1518, he arranges his exposition according to the standards of medieval exegesis, using the *glossa*, both marginal and interlinear, and the *scholia*. To illustrate how Luther at times depends upon this standard and also the terminology of the Scholastics to explain his concepts, we need only look at his lecture on Paul's Epistle to the Romans.

Five times in the *scholia* of the *Römerbriefvorlesung* (1.18; 3.21,23; 5.4; 15.2) Luther refers directly to Peter Lombard, calling him the "Master of Sentences" *(Magister Sententiarum)*[73], and in one place he has this to say concerning the *Sentences:* "Those who

---

71) WA, 9.29 ff.
72) Ibid., 2.414.22. "Ego scio et confiteor, me aliud nihil dixicisse quam ignorantiam peccati, iustitiae, baptismi et totius Christianae vitae, nec quid virtus dei, opus dei, gratia dei, iustitia dei, fides, spes, charitas sit ... Ego Christum amiseram illic, nunc in Paulo reperi."
73) Later in the *Hebräerbriefvorlesung* Luther quotes Lombard by name in 1.5, and refers to the "Master of Sentences" in 7.4,12; 9.24; 11.1.

are robust and perfect may discuss the first book of the *Sentences,* which should be the last rather than the first book" [74]. And in his *Corollarium* to Romans 1.24 (Wherefore God gave them up to the desires of their own hearts) Luther refers to Occam, Lombard, Gabriel Biel, and Pierre d'Ailly. Moreover he uses the medieval terminology in the use of *Respondetur* [75].

Luther's use of the Scholastic method and concepts certainly does not mean that he is always in agreement with them. Particularly on the doctrine of sin, Luther is very critical of the Scholastics. In the *corollarium* to Romans 4.7 (Blessed are those whose iniquities are forgiven and whose sins are covered), Luther states that

> "If this is so, then I must say that I never understood or that the Scholastics did not deal satisfactorily with sin and grace. For they imagine that original sin, just like actual sin, is entirely removed ... The ancient Holy Fathers, Augustine and Ambrose, dealt with these issues quite differently, namely, according to the mode of the Holy Scripture. But the Scholastics follow the mode of Aristotle in his *Ethics* and he places sin and righteousness on works and likewise their position and privation" [76].

Commenting further on this verse on the following page, Luther strikes out at the Scholastics with the term "Sawtheologien" (O fools, O pig-theologians) [77].

Luther is continually lashing out with fury against the Scholastic semi-Pelagianistic concept of sin and grace. In one of his corollaries to Romans (4.7) Luther attacks Peter d'Ailly when he says that "It is ineptly and foolishly said: God has obliged us to have grace and therefore to do what is impossible" [78]. In the *Hebräerbrief-vorlesung* (9.14) he continues his attack when he says,

> "Thirdly, 'to serve the living God'. It follows from this that apart from Christ a man cannot serve the living God, but rather serves

---

74) WA, 56.400.10. "Discutiant primum Sententiarum robusti et perfecti, qui merito non primus, sed novissimus liber esse."

75) Ibid., 56.181.24 ff.

76) Ibid., 56.273.2. "Quae cum ita sint, aut ego nunquam intellexi, aut non bene satis de peccato et gratia theologi scolastica sunt locuti, qui originale totum auferri somniant sicut et actuale, ... cum Augustinus, Ambrosius, multum aliter sint locuti ad modum Scripturae, illi autem ad modum Aristotelis in Ethicorum, qui peccata et iustitiam collocare in opera et eorum positionem et privationem similiter."

77) Ibid., 56.274.14. "O Stulti, O Sawtheologien."

78) Ibid., 56.278.25. "Inepta et stulta est locutio: Deus obligavit nos ad gratiam habendam, ergo ad impossibile."

creatures or idols ... Therefore again, that view which claims it is possible to serve God and do no sin apart from grace is destroyed" 79.

We see in Luther's early exegesis a certain uniqueness. He, unlike Erasmus, used the Scholastic method and quotes their concepts extensively. Yet his uniqueness lies in the way he is able to argue with them and though using their terminology, he is able to expound his own theological concepts in a fresh and different way. His explanation of original sin in his *Römerbriefvorlesung* (5.14) is a good illustration of his use of the structure of the Scholastics while at the same time bringing a new and different meaning to the term:

"Consequently, what now is original sin? First, according to the subtle definition of the Scholastic theologians, it is privation or absence of original righteousness. For according to them righteousness is only subjective in the will, and so therefore its opposite, privation. This, namely, is the category of quality according to Aristotle in his *Logic* and *Metaphysics*. Secondly, but according to the Apostles' honest understanding of Jesus Christ it is not only the privation of quality in the will, nor the loss of light in the intellect, nor power in memory, but, to sum up, the loss of all uprightness and power of all men, body, and soul, and inner and outer man ... Therefore the ancient sacred fathers were correct when they said that original sin itself is the spark or tinder of sin, the law of the flesh, the law of our members, the weakness of nature, a tyrant, the original disease, etc ... Original sin is dealt with by no one so clearly as Gerard Groot in his tract "Beatus Vir" where he speaks not as a thoughtless philosopher, but as a sane and healthy theologian" 80.

---

79) Ibid., 57.209.28. "Tertio ad serviendum Deo viventi. Ex quo sequitur evidenter, quod sine Christo non 'servitur Deo viventi', sed vel creaturis vel idolis ... Unde iterum destruitur sententia, quae dicit servire posse Deo sine gratia et non peccare."

80) Ibid., 56.312.1. "Quid ergo nunc est peccatum originale? Primo secundum subtilitates scolasticorum theologorum est privatio seu carentia iustitie originalis. Justitia autem secundum eos est in voluntate tantum subjective, ergo et privatio eius opposita. Quia sc. est in predicamento qualitatis secundum logicam et methaphysicam. Secundo autem secundum Apostolum et simplicitatem sensus in Christo Jhesu est non tantum privatio qualitatis in voluntate, immo nec tantum privatio lucis in intellectu, virtutis in memoria, sed prorsus privatio universe rectitudinis et potentie omnium virium tam corporis quam anime ac totius hominis interioris et exterioris ... Igitur sicut antiqui patres sancti recte dixerunt: Peccatum illud originis est ipse fomes, lex carnis, lex membrorum, languor naturae, tyrannus, morbus originis etc. ... Hanc originalis peccati apud nullum inveni tam claram resolutionem quam apud Gerardum Groot in tractatulo suo 'Beatus vir', ubi loquitur non ut temerarius philosophus, sed ut sanus theologus."

From this illustration of Luther we can see explicitly what is only implicit in Erasmus' works, i. e., that Luther, by his great knowledge of the Scholastics, used them to help his exposition, while Erasmus rarely quotes them, but usually satirizes their method and theology. In the above illustration Luther has used his fine grasp of *Dogmengeschichte*, the classics, and the Scriptures to develop his doctrine of original sin.

That Erasmus represents a movement away from the Middle Age method of interpretation in his use of *ad fontes* is easy to comprehend, since he was expressedly attempting to break away from the Scholastic system in every way possible. But the difference in the understanding of the term *ad fontes* between Erasmus and the Reformers has more subtle connotations, since both Erasmus and the Reformers had an expressed interest in *ad fontes*.

Erasmus could say along with the Reformers that nothing was as important to him as the Holy Scriptures [81]. In this conception of sacred Scripture as the primary source we see the basic principle that was to unite Erasmus with the Reformation. For both the Reformers and Erasmus saw the Scriptures as the way to bring about the reforms of the church that each in his own way desired. And Luther was pleased with Erasmus' attempt at reform. In a letter to John Lang dated March 1, 1517, Luther states that he is reading Erasmus ... "and it pleases me that he constantly and eruditely condemns both monks and priests for their inveterate ways and stupid ignorance" [82].

But the Christian Humanism of Erasmus and the concepts of Luther were too far apart for these two mutually exclusive ideals ever to be reconciled. As Luther found out, what *ad fontes* meant to Erasmus and what it meant to himself were two dissimilar concepts and ideas. The letter just quoted has much more to say when it is viewed more fully and in its proper context:

"I am reading Erasmus and my esteem for him diminishes daily. It pleases me that he constantly and eruditely condemns both monks and

---

81) Allen, 181.24. "Dici non queat, optime Colete, quam velis equisque properem ad sacras literas, quam omnia mihi fastidio sint quae illinc auocant aut etiam remorantur."

82) WA (Briefwechsel), 1.90.16. "Placet quidem, quod tam religioses quam sacerdotes non minus constanter quam erudite arguit et damnat inveteratae huius et veternosae inscitiae; ..."

priests for their inveterate and stupid ignorance; but I fear that he does not promote Christ nor the grace of God, of which he is more ignorant than is Faber Stapulensis. With him the human is more prevalent than the divine. Though I prefer not to judge him, I admonish you not to read all his works, or rather, do not receive them without judgment" [83].

This letter points out that Luther soon saw that in spite of their points of agreement, Erasmus was humanistically oriented and a reconciliation between them was never possible. Moreover Luther had hints as early as 1516 that he and Erasmus were not cut from the same theological pattern when he wrote to George Spalatin that Erasmus did not understand what Paul meant in Romans 5; that apparently Erasmus had not read Augustine, "On the Spirit and the Letter" [84].

Though both Luther and Erasmus turned to the Scripture as the final authority, their personalities differed to such a large degree that Luther saw the more dogmatic Augustine as the best of the ancients [85] while Erasmus chose the undogmatic Jerome as his champion. This personality difference contributed as much to the disparity in their thinking as did their divergent theories of interpretation.

Being quick to notice the differences between Erasmus and himself, Luther was also able to see Erasmus' positive contributions,

---

83) Ibid., 1.90.15. "Erasmus nostrum lego, et in dies decresit mihi animus erga eum; placet quidem, quod tam religiosos quam sacerdotes non minus constanter quam erudite arguit et damnat inveteratae huius et veternosae inscitiae; sed timeo, ne Christum et gratiam Dei non satis promoveat, in qua multo est quam Stapulensis ignorantior: humana praevalent in eo plus quam divina. Quanquam invitus eum iudico, facio tamen ut te praemoneam, ne omnia legas, imo accipias sine iudicio."

84) Ibid., 1.4. "Quae me in Erasmo, homine eruditissimo, movent, haec sunt, mi Spalatine, quod in apostolo interpretando iustitiam operum seu legis seu propriam (ita enim appellat apostolus) intelligit ceremoniales illas et figurales observantias, deinde de peccato originali (quod utique admittit) non plane velit apostolum loqui cap. V ad Romanos. Qui si legerit Augustinam in eis libris, quos contra Pelagianos scripsit, praesertim de spiritu et litera, ... Ego sane in hoc dissentire ab Erasmo non dubito, quod Augustino in scripturis interpretandis tantum posthabeo Hieronymum, quantum ipse Augustinum in omnibus Hieronymo posthabet."

85) In his Römerbriefvorlesung (WA 56) Luther is to refer to Jerome twelve times and Augustine more than a hundred.

particularly in Erasmus' contribution in leading men back to the Scriptures *(ad fontes)*. To Eoban Hess he wrote,

> "There has never been a great revelation of the word of God unless He has first prepared the way by the resurgence and prospering of languages and letters, as though they were John the Baptists" [86].

In a letter to Oecolampadius he specifically mentions Erasmus in this context,

> "Erasmus has recalled the world from godless studies and reinstated the ancient languages, though, like Moses, he could not himself enter the promised land" [87].

Luther appreciated and used the philological method that Erasmus developed from *ad fontes*, but Erasmus' use of the term itself was too broad for Luther, since he considered the Scriptures as the only true source [88]. *Sola Scriptura* was to become the by-word of the Reformation, not the *ad fontes* of Erasmus.

---

86) Ibid., 3.50.23 (March 29, 1523). "Quin video, nunquam fuisse insignem factam verbi Dei revelationem, nisi primo, velut praecursoribus Baptistis, viam pararit surgentibus florentibus linguis et literis."

87) Ibid., 96.17 (June 20, 1523). "Linguas introduxit et a sacrilegis studiis avocavit. Forte et ipse cum Mose in campestribus Moab morietur."

88) Ibid., 8.236.9. "Es ist auf Erden kein klarer Buch geschrieben denn die Heiligen Schrift, die ist gegen alle andern Bücher gleich wie die Sonne gegen die Licht."

Chapter II

THE AUTHORITY OF THE SOURCES DETERMINED BY THE *PHILOSOPHIA CHRISTI*

It is not feasible to speak of Erasmus' grounding his interpretation of Scripture in Christ, for Christ is not the ground of Erasmus' thought, but rather the goal. It is interesting to note that where today we speak of the person and work of Christ, Erasmus speaks of Christ's actions and ethics; where we speak of Christology, Erasmus speaks of the philosophy of Christ; where we speak of the humanity of Christ, Erasmus speaks of his divinity.

With all the theological emphasis of his day toward a principle of static dogmatism, Erasmus saw in Christ the simple Christianity that was to restore the Christian message to its pure and original form. In this simple Christ he found the aim, goal, and end of the Christian life and ethic.

This concept of the *philosophia Christi*, as well as the other important points of the Erasmian reform, were part of Erasmus' reflections in a relatively early period of his life and did not come during his period of controversy. Erasmus, in the *Enchiridion*, states, "Indeed think of Christ not as an empty word, but nothing else but love, simplicity, patience, purity ..." [1]. The essence of the *philosophia Christi* are these ideals of love, simplicity, and purity. Erasmus envisioned Christ as the incarnation of these ideals. The *philosophia Christi* is the means by which Erasmus wished to bring these ideals into practice and life.

Again and again we see Erasmus appealing to men to follow this simple Christ [2]. He saw in the *philosophia Christi* a return to the

---

1) Holborn, 63.11. "Christum vero esse puta non vocem inanem, sed nihil aliud quam caritatem, simplicitatem, patientiam, puritatem, breviter quicquid ille docuit."

2) "Paraclesis", Holborn, 146.21. "Cur statim malumus ex hominum litteris Christi sapientiam discere quam ex ipso Christo?"
Cf. ibid., 140.8. "Ac primum quidem non libet in praesentia refricare querelam illam non omnino novam, sed heu nimium iustam, et haud scio an unquam iustiorem quam hisce temporibus, cum tam ardentibus animis in sua quisque

simple rational classical Christianity for which he longed. For Erasmus finds this *philosophia Christi* in the Scriptures themselves [3], not in speculation or philosophizing [4]. Erasmus was certainly no mystic. *Ad fontes, philosophia Christi* — over and over the Erasmian reform comes from his pen. It is almost impossible to speak of one without speaking of the other. But it is a rational approach based on the principle of erudition, and the reformation principle of justification by faith was to devour this rational approach in its tide and sweep it out to sea.

Of course, Erasmus shows the principle of justification by faith in his philosophy [5], but never with the boldness or conviction of Luther. Nor is this justification a real act of God's redemption as for Luther, but it is based on Humanistic concepts and principles. That is to say, man climbs out of the cave into light, as Plato would

---

studia mortales incumbant, hanc unam Christi philosophiam a nonnullis etiam Christianis rideri, a plerisque negligi, a paucis tractari, sed frigide; non enim dicam insincere."
Cf. Allen, 512.11. "Novum Textamentum tibi, hoc est viro tum integro tum erudito, proberi non moleste fero; de quo tamen ipse nihil ausim profiteri nisi nos annixos pro virili vt qualicumque industriola nostra Christi philosophiam bonis mentibus commendaremus."
Cf. *Enchiridion*, Holborn, 31.1. "Quod candidum, nulla mortalium doctrina est, quae non sit aliquo nigrore erroris vitiata, sola Christi doctrina tota nivea, tota candida, tota sincera est."

3) *Des. Erasmus Roterodamus Pio Lectori S. D.*, LB vii. "In huius igitur libris verentur omnes, qui venantur christianam philosophiam."
"Paraclesis", Holborn, 149.8. "at hae tibi sacrosanctae mentis illius vivam referunt imaginem ipsumque Christum loquentem, sanantem, morientem, resurgentem, denique totum ita praesentem reddunt, ut minus visurus sis, si coram oculis conspicias."
Ratio ... ad veram Theologiam, Holborn, 304.35. "At si quis magis cupit instructus esse ad pietatem ad disputationem, statim ac potissimum versetur in fontibus, versetur in his scriptoribus, qui proxime biberunt de fontibus."
"Paraclesis", Holborn, 146.23. "..., in his litteris praecipue praestat, in quibus nobis etiamnum vivit, spirat, loquitur, paene dixerim efficacius, quam cum inter homines versaretur. Minus videbant, minus audiebant Iudaei, quam tu vides et audis in euangelicis litteris. ..."

4) Ibid., 145.34. "Neque enim ob id, opinor, quisquam sibi Christianus esse videatur, si spinosa molestaque verborum perplexitate de instantibus, de relationibus, de quidditatibus aut formalitatibus disputet, sed si quod Christus docuit et exhibuit, id teneat exprimatque."

5) *Paraphrases*, LB vii, Romans 1:13. "Evangelium autem voco, iustificationem per fidem in Jesum Christum filium Dei, quem lex promisit et praefiguravit."

see it. Man can, in a sense, redeem himself by his faith or piety. The dynamic thrust of Luther's justification by faith cannot be found in Erasmian or Humanistic thought. Only the words are there, not the power behind the words. For Erasmus, as well as the other Humanists, man is too great in his own right to have to rely totally and absolutely on God for salvation. The absolute sovereignty of God that Calvin stresses so fully can never be found in the writings of an Erasmus. It is this Humanistic approach, based on a rational application, that was to be the underlying factor behind the Erasmian reform.

The *philosophia Christi* that Erasmus pictures as the message of the New Testament is a philosophy of that which Erasmus felt religion should be. It has Christ as its center, but the roads leading to the center are many. There is piety, which Erasmus envisioned as love, simplicity and purity. There is the rational aspect that gives man an important place in achieving this goal. And then there is the idealistic conception that the road to the philosophy of Christ must pass through the great ideals of classicism. In a sense all these roads lead backward; backward to the simple Christ of the Gospels, backward to classicism, and the road to knowledge has its backward movement because it is in the sources that we acquire our knowledge.

In attempting to free the world of what he felt were the excesses of the dogmatic and sterile principles of the Scholastic method, Erasmus' *philosophia Christi* neglected the work of Christ and elevated the person of Christ to the real focal point. The deeds and the acts of Christ with people became the ideals of a true piety [6], but these were focused on the simple and pure Christ that Erasmus

---

6) *Ratio ... ad veram Theologiam*, Holborn, 234.8. "At haec omnia nobis est Christus, et iustitia et pax et sapientia, ..."
Allen, 1062.19. To Lorenzo Campegio. "Olim credebatur philosophia Christiana, non disputabatur; et pia simplicitas hominum sacrorum voluminum oraculis erat contenta: nec egebat variis praescriptis vltro prompta charitas, omnia credens, nusquam haerens."
Des. Erasmus Roterodamus Pio Lectori S. D., LB vii. "Populus sese componat ad studium verae pietatis, et consentientibus pariter atque ardentibus votis sollicitet Jesum Christum, ut principum animos vertat ad consilia pacis. Principes autem, praesertim ecclesiastici, sic instituant consiliorum rationes, ut sincera conscientia non aliud moliantur, quam ut per fidem, caritatem, pietatem, concordiam, per rerum mundanarum contemptum, per rerum coelestium amorem, quam latissime regnet, floreat et imperet Christus."

saw in the New Testament, and not on a Christ that has reconciled the world to God.

Erasmus was impressed by the divinity of Christ rather than his humanity; the concept of a Jesus Christ, truly God, truly man, was foreign to him. Erasmus has a section in *Ratio ... ad veram Theologiam* [7] devoted to explaining and defending the divinity of Christ. The divinity of Christ was so important for Erasmus and his concept of the philosophy of Christ that in pointing out its importance, he relegated the humanity of Christ to a place of secondary importance. The emphasis rests on the pureness and love of this divine Christ.

These facts influenced Erasmus toward a philosophy of Christ rather than toward a theology of Christ. A theology must necessarily include the work of Christ, but a philosophy could concentrate on the ideals of Christ and the working toward bringing these ideals into being. Moreover this philosophy was able to concentrate on the simplicity and pureness of Christ, while a theology must, by its very nature, include more of the dogmatic concepts surrounding this Christ.

The *philosophia Christi* places piety above theology. The important feature for Erasmus was religion and not theology. By religion, Erasmus meant practicing the Christian faith and piety. The philosophy of Christ was that man should live in accordance with the principles set forth in the Gospels. A true Christian is one who *"adorandus ille Christianae philosophiae princeps"* [8].

"There are two things that Christ desires of men: love and faith" [9]. This is truly a call to the *simplicitas Christi*. It is a call to undogmatic Christianity. "The demands of Christ on the Christian conscience are not demands of knowledge, but of morals, or, if I were to speak theologically, with the heart rather than understanding" [10]. The ethical aspect is of prime importance in the *philosophia Christi* [11].

---

7) Holborn, 215.32 ff.

8) *Epicureus,* LB i, 888 c.
Cf. *Enchiridion,* Holborn, 30.17. "Tutissimum est pietatis officiis occupari, ut opera tua non ad terrena studia, sed ad Christum referantur."

9) *Ratio ... ad veram Theologiam,* Holborn, 237.17. "Duo quaedam peculiariter et perpetuo inculcat Christus, fidem et caritatem."

10) *Antibarbarorum Liber,* LB x, 1722 b. "istas mysticas appellationes non ad scientiam, sed ad mores esse referendas, hoc est (ut magis theologice dicam) non ad intellectum, sed ad affectum."

It is in Erasmus' conception of the *philosophia Christi* that we glimpse the personality of Erasmus so clearly. He projects into this philosophy of Christ his own ideals of pureness and simplicity. Furthermore, in the rational aspects, coupled with his desire to go to the sources in order to find this philosophy of Christ, we see the two themes of the Erasmian reform being reiterated time and time again: *bonae litterae, philosophia Christi.* In continually advocating a rational approach grounded in the sources, Erasmus has neglected the concept of revelation, therefore making his philosophy of Christ little more than an ethic. It is a Humanistic ethic at that. This Humanistic aspect is to be a prime force underlying his theory of interpretation. Of course, Erasmus is attempting to guide people to Christ through this *philosophia Christi*, but the attempt is limited by these factors.

One can readily see the implications of such thinking. Everything is subject to the philosophy of Christ and its presuppositions. Even the authority of the sources is, in the final analysis, determined by the *philosophia Christi*.

This formulation of the *philosophia Christi* has a direct effect on Erasmus' theory of interpretation. In his *Novum Testamentum Praefationes* Erasmus states the principle of the philosophy of Christ: "What is the *philosophia Christi*, that He calls *renascentia*, but the insaturation of nature created good? Moreover, no one has taught us so absolutely and effectively as Christ, yet also in pagan books much can be found that is in accord with it" [12].

The crux of this Humanistic statement points out that Erasmus has a natural theology based on natural revelation. This is wedded to the highest form of religion, which he sees in Christ, therefore producing the *philosophia Christi*. Even though Christ himself remains the highest and most absolute religious principle, man has available the best of the classical writing to help him achieve his goal.

---

11) Allen, 189.6. "Ego id etiam in animo verso, quemadmodum possim id quod mihi superest aeui totum pietati, totum Christo impartire."

12) "Paraclesis", Holborn, 145.5. "Quid autem aliud est Christi philosophia, quam ipse renascentiam vocat, quam instauratio bene conditae naturae? Proinde quamquam nemo tradidit haec absolutius, nemo efficacius quam Christus, tamen permulta reperire licet in ethnicorum libris, quae cum huius doctrina consentiant."

The Sacred Scripture is the highest and most absolute ideal of all the sources, but as long as Erasmus has a concept of natural revelation, or to use his own words, that he sees much in accordance with the teachings of Christ in other writings, the Sacred Scriptures lose some of their importance. For Erasmus the Bible never becomes all in all because of his Humanistic and anthropological concept of God and man, faith and piety, classics and Scripture. Man always has his place in the theology of Erasmus and, therefore, in the interpretation of Scripture. The problem of authority is answered by man, with the *philosophia Christi*, a concept conceived and promulgated by Erasmus as the determining factor.

Not only the authority of the sources but also the authority and differentiation of the Scriptures themselves fall under the *philosophia Christi*. This is contrary to the idea that the Church Fathers determine the problem of authority of the Scriptures. The Church Fathers have an important place in the thought of Erasmus, as we shall see in Chapter III, and one cannot speak of the hermeneutic of Erasmus without devoting a section to the place of these men in Erasmus' theory of interpretation. But the fact remains that the Church Fathers are enlighteners and clarifiers of the Holy Text rather than the determining authority for Erasmus.

The *philosophia Christi*, because it is the ultimate for Erasmus, determines the authority of the Bible [13]. Anything that Erasmus sees as agreeing with the philosophy of Christ, as we saw when speaking of the authority of the sources, is very important to Erasmus, but on the other hand, anything that is not in accordance with this *philosophia Christi* is relegated to a subordinate position. The *philosophia Christi* in itself demands selection and rejection. Selection and elevation of all that is in agreement with it, and rejection of all that is not in accordance with the philosophy of Christ. This is the reasoning that Erasmus uses to expound his *philosophia*

---

13) *Praefatio tertae Editionis Novi Testamenti*, LB vi, Anno MDXXIV. "Hanc Philosophiam licebit ex his haurire fontibus, ab hac Christiani vocamur."
Des. Erasmus Pio Lectori S. D., LB vii. "Quamquam in libris evangelicis divina sapientia se mire demittat ad captum etiam infirmorum, ut nemo tam indoctus esse possit, quin ad evangelicam philosophiam sit docilis. Tantum adsit animus, quantumvis rudis, modo simplex, modo purus, ac vacuus ab iis curis et cupiditatibus, quae doctissimos etiam Christo reddunt indociles."
Ibid., "Cupit Christus suam philosophiam quam latissime propagari."

Christi and it is why the *philosophia Christi* and not the Church Fathers determines the place of authority for Erasmus.

Erasmus' view of the Old Testament clarifies the problem of authority in Erasmus' thought. In his view of the Old Testament, the humanism of Erasmus is always in the foreground. But his humanism is interrelated with his *Weltanschauung*.

The ancient civilizations of Egypt, Babylonia, and Syria, or for that matter, Israel, were never considered as important to Erasmus as were the civilizations of Rome and Greece [14]. The cause for this lay in the fact that these more ancient periods were not open to him as were the classical periods. Therefore, when Erasmus says that he wishes an age built on the best of antiquity, he envisions a return to the culture of Rome and Greece rather than a return to the earlier golden age of the Middle East.

Our age is so different from Erasmus' time that it is difficult to envision the thinking of the Middle Ages on the point in question. With the many archeological discoveries of the past hundred plus years our knowledge of the ancient societies is startlingly more profuse than was the Middle Age's. The Middle Age man did not have the advantage of the manuscripts, art, and archeological discoveries that we have available today. To say that the Middle Age knowledge of these ancient periods was clouded by darkness is an understatement, for it was also clouded by myths and superstition, thereby making the few ascertainable facts of doubtful value. The oriental mind and its ideas were alien to the Middle Ages and their gifts to the world little understood and little utilized. Erasmus himself was under the same impressions as his age, and therefore did not understand the real life and culture of these ancient peoples. To him the people of the Old Testament are little more than barbarians.

---

14) It is interesting to note that Erasmus uses the Old Testament biblical illustrations of the evil of Egypt and Babylon freely in the *Enchiridion*, yet he is very hesitant to use illustrations that would hint at the inherent evil that is in paganism per se.

See *Enchiridion*, Holborn, 58.7. "Sic deserenda Aegyptus, ne quando redeas animo ad ollas carnium (Ex. 16:3)." 58.11. "Clamat propheta, ut fugiamus de medio Babylonis. Exitus ab Aegypto fuga vocatur (Jer. 51:6). E Babylone fugere iubemur, non sensim atque cunctanter emigrare."

Cf. *De Contemptu Mundi, LB* v, 1250 e. "ex ista Babylone terra insomniorum umbrarumque plena evolare quod potes propera . . ."

But Erasmus also has a peculiar feature that is different from the general Middle Age conception of the ancient society, and also different from the Renaissance thought. This difference is that although Erasmus was very definitely a Renaissance man, he expressed little interest in the art of the Renaissance or in the leading personalities that produced that art. Erasmus was in contact with such great exponents and masters of the Italian Renaissance art as Michelangelo and Leonardo da Vinci, and also with such leading artists north of the Alps as Hans Holbein and Albrecht Durer; yet he seems unimpressed by them, for he hardly has an allusion to their work in his writings unless that work was connected with him personally.

The new scientific theories of his age, along with the new discoveries of continents, both of which were to have such a profound influence on Western civilization, were of little importance to him, judging from the lack of any references to these in his correspondence. Not only were they unimportant, but Erasmus seems to have had no comprehension of the significance of such events.

Erasmus' letters are one of the primary sources for understanding the thinking of his day, and for understanding the late Middle Ages, in particular the Renaissance movement, yet Erasmus gives few descriptions of the places he visited.

Erasmus was primarily and foremost a man of letters and his aim and goal was to expound and promote letters. Erasmus' conception of life was based on a culture that was far different from the Middle Age Christian life of his day. This world view was rooted in the classical world. He pictured a world that was full of the grandeur of Rome and Greece into which he could lead his fellow men [15]. This world view was a world of serenity and harmony, a fulfilling of the simplicity and pureness of which he felt represented and was represented by the *philosophia Christi.*

---

15) The *Adagia* is a good illustration of Erasmus' *Weltanschauung*. This collection of sayings from the best of Roman and Greek writing was to help Erasmus' generation to become more cultured and educated. The fact that Erasmus would spend so much time on such a work indicates the importance he attached to his efforts.
See particularly the preface to the first edition of the *Adagiorum Collectanea* (Paris 1500).
Allen, 126.50. To William Blount, Lord Montjoy. "Libenter enim audit quisque quod agnoscit, maxime vero si vetustatis commendatio quedam accedat, si quidem adagia non aliter quam vina ab etate precium accipiunt."

The entire *via antiqua* of classical antiquity had a special appeal for Erasmus. He saw there a period of glamour that would transform the drabness of the Middle Ages, if only its truths could be promulgated. He saw this ancient culture as a glorious period that we would term today a time of "gracious living". It is a narrow view because it fails to take into consideration the period preceding and following this *via antiqua*. But this view conditions all of Erasmus' ideas concerning life, its purpose and ideals.

There is therefore a direct relationship between culture and Christianity for Erasmus. Though the *via antiqua* and Christianity were not synonyms for Erasmus, nevertheless his picture of what real Christianity was is definitely tied to what he envisioned in this classical period. It is, as it were, an assimilation of the classical and Christian world. Or it could be called a selection method based on the very best of these ways of life. It is this form of thinking that was so important in producing the ultimate of Erasmus' ideals: the *philosophia Christi*.

Because of these factors Erasmus has very little understanding of the Old Testament. His was a high regard for the Old Testament, both as the background of Christianity and as a source book of Christianity, but he was limited in his ability to comprehend its full meaning and significance [16]. It is therefore no wonder that he never considered it on the same level as the New Testament. The *philosophia Christi* and its ideals of love, purity, and gentleness is only glimpsed at irregular and infrequent intervals in the Old Testament.

Erasmus' efforts in the John Reuchlin controversy illustrates the fact that Erasmus' ideals are more important to him than the Old Testament, and if he must choose between the two, he will without hesitation choose his ideals, which have their fulfillment in the *philosophia Christi*.

John Reuchlin (1455—1522) was, as Erasmus, one of the greatest of the northern Humanists. He was well educated and the first great German, Greek, and Hebrew scholar. His primary interest was Hebrew and he published a Hebrew grammar in 1506 entitled *De rudimentis hebraicis libri tres*. Not only was he interested in

---

16) *Sileni Alcibiabides* (Adagia 1515), LB ii, 773 d. "Etenim ut de Veteri loquamur Instrumento, si praeter historiam nihil spectes, et audias Adam e limo conditum ... nonne putes ex Homeri officina profectam fabulum? ... At sub his involucris, Deum immortalem! quam splendida latet sapientia."

the Old Testament, but he was also very much interested in all Hebrew literature.

When an order from the Kaiser came calling for the destruction of the Rabbinical literature, Reuchlin defended this literature in a work entitled *Oculare Speculum*, thereby involving himself in a dangerous situation. He not only made a magnificent defense of Jewish literature, showing its importance, but he attacked John Pfefferkorn, a converted Jew who was instrumental in gaining the Kaiser's edict against the Rabbinical writings.

Erasmus was very much perturbed over this attack upon his friend Reuchlin [17], although he did not enter the struggle actively as did Reuchlin, nevertheless he defended Reuchlin, even to the point of endangering himself, for he requested Pope Leo X to intercede on Reuchlin's behalf [18].

However it is in Erasmus' letters, especially the ones that were never edited by Erasmus or authorized for publication, that we see the true thinking of Erasmus [19]. In these letters we perceive an openness and frankness of expression and thought that is often omitted in the authorized publications of his letters.

---

17) See the colloquy *Apotheosis Reuchini Capionis*, LB i, 689 c—692 c. "De incomparabili heroe Johanne Reuchlino."
Also, Allen, 1141.13. "Non conquiescent donec linguas ac bonas literas omnes subuerterint. Iam Capionem rursus aggrediuntur, tantum odio Lutheri: qui me dissuadente nomen illius suo negocio admiscens, et illum degrauauit inuidia, et sibi nihil omnio profuit."

18) Ibid., 335.303. "Inter quos est eximius ille vir. Ioannes Reuchlinus Phoecensis, trium linguarum Graecae, Latinae et Hebraicae paene ex aequo peritus; ad haec in nullo doctrinae genere non ita versatus vt cum primus certare possit. Vnde merito virum hunc ceu phoenicem et vnicum suum decus tota suspicit ac veneratur Germania."
Cf. ibid., 333.105. To Raffaelle Riario, Cardinale Sancti Gaeorgii. "Maiorem in modum te et obsecro et obtestor per bonas litteras, quibus tua celsitudo semper vnice fauere solet, vt eximius vir, dominas Iohannes Reuchlinas, in suo negocio aequos vos sentiat et beneuolos."

19) Erasmus authorized several editions of his letters to be published during his lifetime, and he carefully edited these, deleting statements that could be misconstrued or adding statements in order to place himself in a better light in the eyes of the public. In the *Opus Epistolarum Erasmi* we are fortunate to have available many of Erasmus' letters that were never edited or authorized by Erasmus for publication, therefore giving us a clearer picture of Erasmus' true thoughts.
Allen, 1206.5. To Beatus Rhenanus (preface to the *Epistolae ad diueras*). "Cuius aeditionem partim extorsit amicorum flagitatio, partim ipsa necessitas;

In writing to John Caesarius [20], Erasmus, when speaking of Pfefferkorn, says, "For my own part, provided that the New Testament remain intact, I had rather that the Old Testament should be altogether abolished, than that the *peace* of Christiandom should be destroyed for the sake of the books of the Jews" [21].

Erasmus' concern in this controversy points out clearly that he is more interested in his ideals than in the Old Testament itself. This gives weight to the thesis that the problem of authority is determined by Erasmus' ideals, of which the highest ideal is the *philosophia Christi*, rather than by other factors such as the Church Fathers.

The superstition, shadows, and lack of culture in the Old Testament make it pre-Christian in meaning. The ancient superstition which sometimes flows through the passages and stories of the Old Testament covers the truth of the message. This, together with the cruelty and barbaric ways of the peoples represented, presented to Erasmus a lack of culture that was directly opposed to his personal principles of gentleness, simplicity, and the like. As a person who saw the *philosophia Christi* as the way to combat the above-mentioned things that were so abominable to him, it is no wonder that he was never able to give the Old Testament a place equal to the New Testament.

Erasmus' personal principles, or, correctly stated, the application of these principles as set forth in the *philosophia Christi*, was to be the determining factor in authority throughout his life. As late as 1535 and in the last year of his life, he could still say, in *Eccle-*

---

cum viderem accinctos qui quod habebant epistolarum mearum, vel inuito me essent publicaturi. Atque id facturos sese iam palam literis ad me suis minitabantur."

20) Ibid., 701.35. "Malim ego incolumi Novo Testamento vel totum Vetus aboleri quam Christianorum pacem ob Iudeorum libros rescindi."

21) Ibid., 700.14. "Audio pestilentissimum illud granum, quod Satanas aliquis in geniousus seuit, edidisse libellum in quo impune debactatur in doctos omneis. Hoc organo abutuntur praeclari illi religionis professores ad subuertendum tranquil-(l)itatem Christianae concordiae. Vtina(m) ille totus esset Iudeus, aut, sicut habet praepucium amputatum, ita haberet et linquam et manus ambas!

Cf. ibid., 697.11. "Scripunt ad me docti Pepercornium, ex scelerato Iudaeo sceleratissimum Christianum, edidisse librum lingua Germanica, in quo doctos omneis et inter hos me mira rabie lacerat ac discerpit. O pestem indignam talibus adversariis, dignam carnifice! Tanti erat aqua tingi, vt concordiam Christianam personatus Iudaeus turbaret."

siastae, that he preferred the New Testament, where all is clear, plain, and true, and where nothing savors of superstition and cruelty, but all is simplicity and gentleness [22], to the mysteries of the Old Testament, where truth is sometimes covered up in indecent and silly fables [23].

The notion that the Old Testament is filled with shadows over against the light of the New Testament has other significance when we consider the importance that Erasmus places upon erudition. Because of this emphasis on a rational approach to the understanding of Scripture, Erasmus must necessarily relegate the Old Testament to a subordinate position of authority if he is to remain consistent in his approach. Because certain passages were a hindrance to him when trying to exegete or ascertain their meaning, it is natural for Erasmus to disregard these passages or relativize their importance.

It follows that it was easy for Erasmus to accomplish this relativization by making the Old Testament the background of Christianity rather than finding there a continuous working of God toward a fixed purpose: a *Heilsplan*. Erasmus pictures a form of progressive religion rather than *Heilsgeschichte*. For this reason he could write to his friend, Wolfgang Fabricius Capito, that

> "I should wish you were more given to Greek than to Hebrew studies, although I do not condemn the latter ... I wish the Christian Church did not rely so much on the Old Testament, which, although it was given for a certain period of time and is full of shadows, is almost preferred to the Christian writing (the New Testament)" [24].

Because Erasmus saw no *Heilsplan* in the Old Testament, one can easily understand his theory of progression of religion that is

---

22) *Ecclesiastae,* LB v, 1043 c. "Velut si quis per petram, unde Hebraeis in deserto fluxit aqua, neget significatum Christum, aut per Mosis faciem velo obtectam neget significari Judaeos rejicientes Euengelii gratiam, per Christum omnibus referatum."

23) Ibid., 870 c. "Nec oportet Hebraica nomina quamvis non intellecta cum taedio audire, quum in Canonicis litteris ne apex quidem unus temere positus sit: sed quemadmodum thecas rerum sacrarum veneramur, ignari quid intus sit, modo persuasum habeamus factum esse quod occultatur: ita decet ea nomina, quorum omnia mysteria non possumus ad liquidum explicare, cum reverentia vel audire vel recitare."

24) Allen, 798.19. "Optarim te propensiorem ad Graeca quem ista Hebraica, licet ea non reprehendam ... Atque vtinam Christianorum Ecclesia non tantum tribueret Veteri Testamento, quod, cum pro tempore datum

finalized in Christ. So for Erasmus the Christian doctrine becomes the highest form of religion, a religion that is at the same time different from the Old Testament, yet is kin to the Old Testament ideals. For this reason Erasmus could state, "The law of Moses and the prophets is a step toward the evangelical doctrine of Christ" [25].

This theory manifests itself in a very Humanistic form, for Erasmus saw the evangelical teaching as renewing and completing the pureness of the natural world [26]. The wisdom of antiquity is combined with ancient Hebrew law. Natural law or wisdom is combined with revealed law to renew the old concept of *animae naturaliter Christianae*.

After considering such factors as Erasmus' *Weltanschauung* and the other features of Erasmus' thought that make the Old Testament pre-Christian in meaning, it becomes clear why the authority of the Old Testament is included under the chapter that deals with the *philosophia Christi*. Since it is the philosophy of Christ that is the highest ideal for Erasmus, it is natural for him to make everything subservient to it. The Old Testament, though very dear at times to Erasmus, does not measure up to the principles found in this *philosophia Christi*, therefore the Old Testament can never be considered on the same plane as the New Testament.

Erasmus' greatest contribution lies in his propounding of the New Testament. In attempting to lead theology and his age back to the New Testament text itself, Erasmus performed a great service to Christianity. The more one studies Erasmus the more one is convinced that the New Testament occupies the central place in the hermeneutic of Erasmus.

Why is the New Testament so much more important than the Old Testament? Why is the New Testament the most authoritative of all the sources? Because the New Testament is where we find

umbris constet, Christianis litteris pene antefertur: internim vtcunque deflectimus a Christo, qui vel vnus nobis sufficiebat."

25) *Paraphrasis,* LB vii. Romans 3:2. "Siquidem Mosi lex et prophetarum oracula gradus est ad evangelicam Christi doctrinam."
Cf. ibid., Hebrews 13:9. "Non aliud docuit lex mosaica, quam docet evangelium, sed aliter."

26) Ibid., Matthew 19.8. "evangelica doctrina renovat ac perficit naturae sinceritatem."
Cf. ibid., I Cor. 9:8. "Nonne quod naturae ratio dictat, idem et sacra lex jubet."

Christ and his philosophy [27]. As Preserved Smith has remarked, "The purpose of Christianity was to show love ambodied in the person of Christ and enshrined in the New Testament" [28].

The New Testament, Christ, and the *philosophia Christi* are so intermingled in the thought of Erasmus that it is impossible to separate them. It is in the New Testament that we find Christ and his philosophy, yet it is Christ and the *philosophia Christi* that determine the importance of the New Testament. It is paradoxical that Erasmus finds the *philosophia Christi* in the New Testament, while superimposing the same philosophy of Christ on the New Testament. The New Testament is the source of the *philosophia Christi*, nevertheless the *philosophia Christi* determines the authority of the New Testament.

To see this relationship between the New Testament, Christ, and the *philosophia Christi* we need only to turn to Erasmus himself. In the *Novum Testamentum Praefationes*, Erasmus states that he wishes all people to read the gospels and letters of Paul, for Christ desires that his teachings be spread as far as possible. "For are we not all baptized with the same baptism and all profess the same *philosophia Christi?*" [29]

Erasmus was not aware of his error of subordinating the New Testament to the *philosophia Christi*. He saw only that in the New Testament we find Christ and his teachings. This is the positive element that was to have such a profound effect upon the

---

27) "Paraclesis", Holborn, 143.3. "Is mihi vere theologus est, qui non syllogismis arte contortis, sed affectu, sed ipso vultu atque oculis, sed ipsa vita doceat aspernandas opes, ... (Matthew 5—7).
Ibid., 13. "Haec inquam et huiusmodi si quis afflatus spiritu Christi praedicet, inculcet, et haec hortetur, invitet, animet, in demum vere theologus est, etiamsi fossor fuerit aut textor."

28) Preserved Smith, *Erasmus, A Study of his Life, Ideals, and Place in History*. New York and London, 1923. p. 173.

29) "Paraclesis", Holborn, 142.14. "Regum mysteria celare fortasse satius est, at Christus sua mysteria quam maxime cupit evulgari. Optarim, ut omnes mulierculae legant euangelium, legant Paulinas epistolas. Atque utinam haec in omnes omnium linguas essent transfusa, ut non solum a Scotis et Hibernis, sed a Turcis quoque et Saracenis legi cognoscique possint."
Ibid., 28. "Neque enim consentaneum est, cum baptismus ex aequo communis sit Christianorum omnium, in quo prima Christianae philosophiae professio est, ..."
Erasmus says to "put on philosophy of Christ", but Paul in Gal. 3:27 says "as many as are baptized in Christ have put on Christ".

hermeneutic of his day. In seeking to lead men to the New Testament in their quest of Christ and his teachings, Erasmus opened a new door to exegetical study of his day, the consequences far outstripping his naive concept of the *philosophia Christi*.

The New Testament is closely tied in with the concept of piety in the thought of Erasmus. Erasmus envisioned the study of the New Testament as leading to a new piety and therefore toward a purification of the Church. Piety is also an integral part of the *philosophia Christi:*

> "This philosophy is of the heart rather than understanding, of life rather than knowledge, of inspiration rather than erudition, of transformation rather than reason" [30].

These concepts of the New Testament, *philosophia Christi*, and piety go hand in hand, complementing one another, and resulting in a movement toward a reform of the church.

Erasmus was very proud of the fact that his edition of the New Testament met with such instant success. He felt that he had induced people to study the New Testament that never would have done so otherwise [31]. He imagined that his New Testament was to help bring about the much-needed reform of the church, and the years immediately following its publication were his happiest years.

Since the time immediately before the publication of the New Testament heralds the golden era in the life of Erasmus, one can note the enthusiasm and optimism that he possessed at this time. The study of the *Christiana Philosophia* was to lead toward sanctification [32]. The Scriptures should be translated into the vernacular, thereby allowing everyone to move toward a new piety in life [33].

---

30) "Paraclesis", Holborn, 144.35. "Hoc philosophiae genus in affectibus situm verius quam in syllogismis vita magis est quam disputatio, afflatus potius quam eruditio, transformatio magis quam ratio."

31) Allen, 413.3. "Nouum Testamentum cum tibi destinassem, cur mutato consilio summo Pontifici inscripserim, literis meis iampridem exposui: quae tua est humanitas, imo prudentia, boni consulet, spero, quod fecimus. Timebatur hoc opus antequam prodiret; caeterum aeditum mirum est quam probetur omnibus etiam theologis, vel eruditis vel integris et candidis."
Ibid., .29. "Multi legunt hac occasione diuinas literas, nunquam alias lecturi, quod ipsi fatentur; complures graecari coeperunt, imo passim."

32) "Paraclesis", Holborn, 139.6. "At ego sane, si quid huiusmodi votis proficitur, tantisper dum mortales omnes ad sanctissimum ac saluberrimum

Erasmus sums up his aims in publishing his New Testament when he states:

> "So I beseech you, beloved reader, that you bring pious ears and a Christian heart to the reading of this book. Let no man take this work with the same feeling that he would, for example, the *Noctes atticae* of Gellius, or the *Miscellanea* of Politian ... We are in the presence of Holy things; there is no question of eloquence, these matters are best recommended to the world by simplicity and purity; it would be ridiculous to display human erudition here, impious to pride oneself on human eloquence ... in simple and pure zeal we are furnishing these Scriptures for Christian hearing so that in the future more may make use of this sacrosanct philosophy, and all the more willing and with less trouble they may benefit more profitably. May Christ himself, who is our witness and helper in the work we have undertaken, look upon us with disfavor if we seek any reward or gain from our efforts" [34].

When Erasmus writes as he does in the above quote, there can be no doubt as to the authority he gives to the New Testament. *Sacras litteras,* particularly the New Testament, is the highest form of *bonae litterae.* But the fact remains that in the final analysis the New Testament becomes the prey of the Erasmian principle of *philosophia Christi.* Though the authority of the New Testament in the field of literature cannot be questioned, this authority is determined not by the New Testament *ipso verbo,* but by the superimposed principle of the *philosophia Christi* [35].

Christianae philosophiae studium adhortor ac veluti classicum canens evoco, ..."

33) Ibid., 142.10. "Vehementer enim ab istis dissentio, qui nolint ab idiotis legi divinas litteras in vulgi linguam transfusas, sive quasi Christus tam involuta docuerit, ut vix a pauculis theologis possint intelligi, sive quasi religionis Christianae praesidium in hoc situm sit, si nesciatur."

34) Allen, 373.202. "Proinde te, quaeso, lector optime, vt tu quoque vicissim pias aures et Christianum pectus ad legendum adferas. Ne quis haec eo animo in manus sumat quo fortassis sumit Noctes Gellianas aut Angeli Politiani Miscellanea; ... In re sacra versamur, et in ea re quae simplicitate puritateque potissimum est orbi commendata: in qua reidiculum sit humanam eruditionem ostentare velle, impium humanam iactare eloquentiam; ... Simplici puroque studio tradimus haec Christianis auribus, quo posthac in sacrosancta hae philosophia et plures versarentur et lubentius, denique vt minore cum negocio, "ita maiore cum fructu. Christum ipsum, quo teste simul et adiutore molimur haec, parum mihi propitium imprecor, nisi ex hisce laboribus adeo nihil venamur emolumenti, vt magnam etiam certamque rei pecuniariae iacturam scientes ac volentes acceperimus."

35) Allen, 563.17. to Oecolampadius, "nihil in sacris literis praeter Christum quaerendum".

53

It is not our task to formulate or postulate here the authority of the Holy Scriptures for Luther or Calvin. Nevertheless it is interesting to note two points of divergence between the problem of authority for Erasmus and that of Luther and Calvin, in respect to the context of this chapter.

Erasmus viewed the importance of the New Testament and its *philosophia Christi* as lying in its message of piety. Erasmus uses such phrases as believing, holding, and adoring the Scriptures [36]. There is usually the ring of piety connected with his writings. The extended use of the New Testament was to lead to a moral reawakening that would have a profound effect on culture.

This is nowhere near the case with Luther. Luther perceived that the Scriptures held a doctrinal rather than a philosophical value [37]. While Luther was to have a profound influence on the culture of Europe, nevertheless he was not interested in Christianity as a morally uplifting force on culture as such. The Scriptures are the source of the God that forgives man, rather than the source of a philosophy of life that was to morally revitalize mankind. The difference naturally lay in the fact that Erasmus with his humanistic principles conceived of sin as a moral weakness or imperfection, while Luther took sin seriously.

In his work, *Rationis Latomianae confutatio* (1521), Luther is forced to answer directly to charges that his view of sin is contrary to the doctrines of the church. This treatise is particularly interesting for our study for here we see Luther not only grounding his approach in the authority of Scripture, but moreover in direct opposition to the Erasmian concept that Scripture is primarily a moral force. Of course, Luther was interested in Christian obedience, and the tropological sense was very important in his exegetical method, but here the discussion is centered upon the doctrine of sin rather than discipleship, and it is here that we

---

36) *Ratio ... ad veram Theologiam*, Holborn, 298.25. "Nobis satis est credere, tenere, et adorare quod scriptum est."

37) Luther also stresses the Christological interpretation of the Scriptures. As early as his *Römerbriefvorlesung* he stated, "There is opened up to us a broad approach to the understanding of Sacred Scriptures: we must understand it in its entirety with respect to Christ *(tota de Christo sit intelligenda)* particularly where it is prophetic."
WA, 56.59 (glossa). "Hic magnus aperitur introitus in sacre Scripture intelligentiam, sc. quod tota de Christo sit intelligenda, maxime ubi est prophetica."

perceive another radical difference between Erasmus and Luther and the use of the authority that they give to the Scriptures.

In part three of this treatise Luther says that the divine Scriptures deal with our sin in two ways: one, law; two, Gospel. These are the two testaments that God has ordained for our salvation that we may be set free from sin [38]. He continues,

> "Now the law introduced us to sin ... so that we would search to be freed from it and hope for grace. Now the Gospel also declares and teaches both the righteousness and grace of God. Through its righteousness it heals the corruption of our human nature" [39].

The above gives forth a different flavor from the New Testament message that Erasmus placed on such a high plane in his thought. A comparison with Luther accentuates the fact that Erasmus is humanistically oriented to the point that it influences even his idea of the New Testament.

That John Calvin likewise differs from Erasmus on the doctrine of sin is a well-known fact, so let us approach the thought of Calvin in relationship to Erasmus' concept of the Scriptures as a moral force in a different light. Though Calvin, like Luther, had a very strong doctrine of sin, his theology contains an even stronger moral element. For Calvin, "in order for us to be the creatures of God, Scripture must be our guide and teacher" [40]. Of course, this differs widely from Erasmus' concept that Scripture is a morally renewing force, but it shows that Calvin gives a prime place to the moral element contained in the Scriptures.

There is one other point that is interesting to bring into consideration in this chapter and that is the differences that become apparent over the authority of the Old Testament. Erasmus, as we noted earlier, could speak highly of the Old Testament, yet when his principles came under attack he could prefer to discard it, rather than his principles.

---

38) WA, 8.103,35. "Scriptura divina peccatum nostrum tractat duobus modis, uno perlegum dei, altero per Euangelium dei."

39) Ibid., 105.37. "Lex enim introduxit et eos obruit peccato ..., ut ab illo liberari peteremus et gratiam suspiraremus. Nam Euangelium etiam duo praedicat et docet, iustitiam et gratiam dei. Per iustitiam sanat corruptionem naturae ..."

40) Inst., I, 6,1. "Ut ad Deum creatorem quis perveniat, opus esse scriptura duce et magistra."

Both Luther and Calvin felt that both New and Old Testaments were the Word of God (a term foreign to Erasmus) and to speak of the authority of Scripture without considering the Old Testament as well as the New was unthinkable to them.

Luther found Christ in all of Scripture [41], and was worried over the fact that the people of his day were primarily reading the New Testament as if the Old Testament were principally for the Jews [42]. This is quite another thing from the thrust of Erasmus' emphasis on the New Testament where alone Christ is found.

Calvin varies from Luther in emphasis of authority of the Old Testament. The emphasis for Calvin rests on the sovereignty of God. The authority of the Scriptures is grounded in God, because there God is and there God speaks [43]. Furthermore the first point of Christianity is that sacred Scripture is all our knowledge because it is God who speaks there [44].

Of course Calvin, as well as Luther, has much more to say concerning the authority of Scripture, but these passages give us an insight into the differences in their understanding of the authority of the Scriptures and that of Erasmus. And it is their understanding rather than Erasmus' that is accepted by the future. The *philosophia Christi* became a symbol of a bygone age. Such terms as justification by faith and sovereignty of God governed the theology of the Reformation.

---

41) WA, 12.438. "Tota scriptura eo vergit, ut Christum nobis proponat, ut Christum cognoscamus."

42) Ibid., Deutsche Bibel 8.11,1 ff. "Vorrede auf des Alte Testament" (1545).
Cf. ibid., p. 10,1 ff. "Vorrede Martini Luther" (1523).

43) Inst., I, 6,1. "Quanquam autem multa ex Novo Testamento testimonia adhibebimus, alia etiam ex Lege et Prophetis, ubi expressa fit Christi mentio: in hunc tamen finem tendent omnia, Deum mundi opificem nobis patefieri in Scriptura, et quid de eo sentiendum sit exponi, ne per ambages incertam aliquod numen quaeramus."

44) CR. LIV (*Calvini Opera* XXVI), p. 131. "Car ils ne savent pas le premier poinct de la Christientè, c'est que l'Escriture saincte est toute nostre sagesse, et qu'il nous faut escouter Dieu qui parle là, sans y rien adiouster."

Chapter III

ERUDITION AS THE MEANS TO INTERPRETATION

Erasmus was not a theologian [1] by temperament but the nature of his interest in the New Testament text propelled him into the arena of interpretation, which was normally a theologian's task and therefore foreign to a person of Erasmus' interest and learning. In his attempt to restore the biblical text, Erasmus had entered the field of text criticism. Both in working with the text itself (restorer and lexicographer) and in his task of interpretation (the exegetical aspect), Erasmus found himself in the position of text critic. The means that Erasmus saw to the correct method of interpretation and restoration of the Scriptures can be summarized in the term, *eruditio*.

Erudition, for Erasmus, meant a learned grammatical, objective, scientific study of the sources. It is a rational approach, but it denotes more emphasis on learning than reason [2]. The exegesis of the sources stems from a knowledge of them, their language, etc., rather than a reasoning out of their meaning through a system or process. The emphasis is on man's ability to understand the text, but only because he is educated and desires to devote the time and energy to study that is necessary for understanding. This approach is based on humanistic ideals. There is little of the analytical approach that is found in a truly rationalistic approach.

Erasmus' primary interest was in restoring the New Testament text, and his treatment of the text was based on a learned knowledge of it. The New Testament, along with other literature, was to be viewed as literature, and one must have the proper tools to deal literarily with it [3].

---

1) Allen, 1805.94. "Dogmatistae personam semper refugi, nisi quod obiter quaedam admonui quae mihi videbantur corrigendis studiis ac preposteris hominum iuditiis conducere."

2) Ibid., 56.9. "Prima igitur cura sit vt praeceptorem tibi eligas quam eruditissimum."

3) Ibid., 337.862. "Nos vniuersum Testamentum Nouum ad Graecorum exemplaria vertimus, additis e regione Graecis, quo cuius promptum sit con-

The concept of erudition as the means by which we interpret the Scriptures is as profound as it is naive, for it necessarily presupposes and demands an exacting knowledge of the original languages, the complexities of the grammatical structure of the text, and the other proper tools that are so necessary in dealing with the restoration and exegesis of the text.

Scientific erudition, therefore, rather than reason, is the means by which Erasmus interprets Scripture [4]. Scholarship, understanding, enlightenment are the qualities that underline and explain this concept of erudition. It is, as it were, an attempt by man to control the message of the Scriptures through his own efforts. It is anthropocentric, but nevertheless, in the way Erasmus utilized it, it was an effective means of interpretation, for it represented a new, if not different, approach for his day, and helped to open the eyes of scholars to a more flexible and deeper means of exegeting the text.

Knowledge leads to faith [5]. Faith is moreover a completion and conquering of pure knowledge. This type of reflection — that knowledge leads to faith — is rooted in humanism and therefore is the underlying theme of liberalism, because faith is not then the gift of God [6], but rather the ultimate position that man, through knowledge, or his own efforts, can achieve. It is a theologically poor, but historically beneficial position that Erasmus held, for it presented a means to explore the Biblical passages from a standpoint that gave possibilities of emphasis that were strikingly in contrast with the recognized and accepted form of Middle Age or Scholastic exegesis.

Erasmus also felt that erudition as a form of enlightenment was to rid the world of darkness or barbarianism. Here we see both the Erasmian reform asserting itself and the Platonistic idea of light and darkness, good and evil, creeping into the thought of Erasmus. This Platonistic dualism was to lessen the importance of such works

---

ferre. Adiecimus separatim Annotationes, in quibus partim argumentis, partim veterum autoribate theologorum docemus non temere mutatem quod emendauimus, ne vel fide careat nostra correctio vel facile deprauari possit quod emendatum est."

4) *Hyperaspistes,* LB x, 1303 d. "Nec illa Scripturas interpretatum nisi ex eruditorum concilio, . . ."

5) *Enchiridion,* Holborn, 64.10. "Scientia plus affert adiumenti ad pietatem quam forma aut vires corporis aut opes."

6) Ephesians 2.8.

as his *Paraphrasis,* for here, when commenting on the blind man of Luke 18.35, Erasmus went so far as to identify light with faith, and darkness with sin [7].

Since faith for Erasmus is a matter of erudition, and since through learning man can interpret the text, it is easy to see the deficiencies of such a system. Yet the positive value of this system of erudition is also clear, particularly if viewed in the context of the age in which Erasmus lived and worked.

Erudition or learning, though steeped in humanistic ideals and grounded in anthropocentric concepts, was nevertheless an attempt to deal with the sources themselves. If one was to know the sources, one must be scholarly. If one was to be proficient in his use of the text, one must be learned in the ways and language of the text. Knowledge was of primary importance for Erasmus, but the real importance of learning was to help one understand the sources and text of these sources. Erudition in itself is not a principle of Erasmus' thought. Erudition has value only in so far as it helps one to come to a sure knowledge of the sources. Knowledge to understand the text, knowledge in order to help other people understand the text, never abstract knowledge or knowledge for its own sake.

Erudition and *ad fontes* are therefore interrelated. Erudition demands knowledge of the original languages and the grammatical and philological criticism of the text just as *ad fontes* does. *Eruditio* is, in fact, the means that Erasmus used to exegete the *fontes.* The formal principle in the hermeneutic of Erasmus is a learned and scholarly approach to the sources themselves. It is the aim of Erasmus to come to a knowledgeable understanding of the *fontes.* Therefore *eruditio* and *bonae litterae* are synonymous and at times even interchangeable, for as we saw in chapter one, *bonae litterae* in one sense means 'good learning'.

Behind this principle of erudition lie three factors that enabled Erasmus to postulate his theory that correct interpretation of the text is based on a knowledgeable understanding of the text. These three factors are: 1. The text adapts itself to the present situation (relativism); 2. Historical criticism; 3. The utilization of the Church Fathers in exegesis.

---

7) LB vii, Luke 18.35. "Lumen est fides, tenebrae sunt terrenae cupiditates."

In dealing with the New Testament Erasmus saw that a hermeneutical problem existed between sound exegesis and the explanation of the text so that its message is relevant and, especially important for Erasmus, applicable [8]. One illustration of Erasmus' attempt to answer this problem can be found in his two chief works on the New Testament: *In Novum Testamentum omnia cum Annotationes*, and *Paraphrasis in Novum Testamentum*. In the former work Erasmus is primarily exegetical, though not always, and his interest is in setting forth the best text possible. But on the other hand, the *Paraphrasis* is primarily a work of explaining the meaning of the passage in understandable terms, rather than exegeting the text itself.

But the real answer that Erasmus developed to bridge this gap between exegesis and explanation was the principle that the text adjusts or adapts itself to the present situation [9]. In order to view this answer of Erasmus in the context in which Erasmus stated it, we must turn our attention to the facts behind this statement. This is found in the *Hyperaspistis, Liber II*, and is a work written as a defense against Luther's *De servum arbitrium*, which had answered Erasmus' *De libero arbitrio*. A work of this nature must be well-planned and thought-out with great care or it will not fulfill its purpose. We can assume, therefore, that when Erasmus makes this statement that the text adapts itself to the present situation, he knew what he was doing, that this statement is not taken from some obscure writing that Erasmus had hastily prepared and did not actually mean. In other words, we can accept this statement as a genuine principle of Erasmus' theory of interpretation since this is the aim to which it was written.

It is easy to understand the phenomena that led Erasmus to make such a statement. First, there is the debate with Luther over what is the correct theory of interpretation. Then there are the other

---

8) This hermeneutical problem has existed since New Testament times where we see the New Testament writers facing the problem of the use of the Old Testament in their exposition.

9) LB x, 1355 e. "Multa aliter dicturus si in hoc seculum incidisset audissetque meras necessitates, lusus et insultationes, non quod sibi non constet Paulus, sed quod rebus praesentibus *accomodanda* sit oratio."
Cf. Erich Seeberg, *Luthers Theologie*, vol. I, p. 65 (Stuttgart 1937). "Der historische Relativismus des Erasmus formuliert hier (in quote above) übrigens wohl zum erstenmal die von der Aufklärung so bevorzugte 'Akkomodations theorie'."

factors, such as Erasmus' unceasing struggle with the Scholastic theory of interpretation, his hope of an ethic based on the *philosophia Christi*, and his ultimate goal of having all men read and know the Scriptures. The argument with Luther was theological, but the other aims are all involved in promulgating the Erasmian reform, and this in itself meant that the Scriptures must be able to speak out against the abuses of the times.

The practical application of such a theory of adjustment is found throughout Erasmus' writings. Even in the *Annotationes* we see Erasmus advocating his reform. He uses Matthew 11.30 (my yoke is easy and my burden is light) to criticize the many churchly institutions that have been organized since the early church. He envisions these as suffocating the pure and simple message of the 'philosopy of Christ' [10].

Such an approach as Erasmus' theory of the text adapting itself to the present situation naturally stems from such problems as writing from an apologetical viewpoint. With this interest in making the Scriptures historically relevant, Erasmus uses both his *Annotationes* and *Paraphrasis* to promote reform, to tirade against the religious evils of his day, and speak out for piety. In a sense Erasmus lets his age dictate the questions and, in attempting to answer these questions, he follows an apologetic approach.

This apologetical approach that Erasmus uses is not so much in itself a fallacy as the application that he derives from it. In attempting to be relevant, in his application Erasmus relativizes at times the meaning of the Scripture, thereby lessening his value as exegete [11].

The theory that the text adapts itself to the present, though not particularly a good exegetical principle, nevertheless had one value for the exegesis of Erasmus' day in that it helped men to become interested in making the text relevant rather than in defining the meaning of the text, as was the case in Scholasticism with its *glossa* and *scholia*. Erasmus' *Annotationes* and *Paraphrasis* certainly rep-

---

10) LB vi, 63—5; cf. ibid., 117—8 on Matt. 23.5.
Erasmus is not exegeting the passage here and making an application of this exegesis, but he is making the text relevant to the present situation. The sources are no longer speaking for themselves, but have become subject to the period in which they are interpreted.

11) This approach of adapting the text to the present situation alleviates the necessity of sound exegesis in certain passages.

resent a departure from the typical Scholastic commentary and present a fresh if not altogether correct approach.

The second factor that helped Erasmus to hold fast to his principle of *eruditio* was his use of historical criticism. Through the use of an historical approach to the Scripture, Erasmus was given the tools to deal with passages that otherwise would have been too difficult to understand. This historical approach to Scripture also added depth and breadth to his exegesis, thereby adding new understanding to the Biblical passages.

Erasmus' use of historical criticism is set forth in *Ratio ... ad veram theologiam.*

> "One comes nearer to perceiving the sense of Scripture if he considers not only the situation and what is said, but also by whom it is said, to whom it is said, the words that are said, what time, what occasion, what precedes and what follows" [12].

This statement also includes a philological approach, but our interest here is primarily historical criticism, which Erasmus has clearly presented. The situation, the context, writer and reader, all the elements of historical criticism are included.

Another feature of Erasmus' historical critical method was that he wished to interpret the more obscure passages in the light of the passages that were clear [13], and if a person stumbled over difficulties in interpreting certain passages that seemed contrary to each other, that person should not be shocked or doubt what is written, but he should search for the explanation of the difficulty in consideration of the whole context [14]. Erasmus also conscien-

---

12) *Ratio ... ad veram theologiam*, Holborn, 196.29. "Accedet hinc quoque lucis nonnihil ad intelligendum scripturae sensum, si perpendamus non modo quid dicatur, verum etiam a quo dicatur, cui dicatur, quibus verbis dicatur, quo tempore, qua occasione, quid praecedat, quid consequatur."
Cf. ibid., 185.6. "Iam si gentium, apud quas res gesta narratur, sive ad quas scribunt apostoli, non situm modo, verum etiam originem, mores, instituta, cultum, ingenium ex historicorum litteris didicerimus, ..."

13) Ibid., 291.24. "His in ordinem compositis iuxta rerum pugnantiam aut affinitatem (ut in Copia quoque nostra quondam indicavimus) quicquid usquam insigne est in omnibus veteris instrumenti libris, in euangeliis, in Actis, in litteris apostolorum, quod vel conveniat vel dissonet, ad hos erit redigendum."

14) Ibid., 215.27. "Huiusmodi scrupi si quando inciderint, non oportebit offendi aut de fide scripti dubitare, sed pensitatis omnibus circumstantiis explicandae difficultatis rationem quaerere."

tiously examined and estimated the codices after date and worth of each [15]. His judgments proved to be not too reliable, but in his method we have the foundations of modern historical criticism.

This historical critical approach is an effort on the part of Erasmus to understand and grasp more fully the meaning of the text itself. In asking the questions about the situation, writer, purpose, context, and interpreting passages by others that are clear, Erasmus is not attempting a theological study, but rather a deeper understanding of the text itself. Historical criticism is an erudite attempt by Erasmus to deal with the text and not an effort at theological meaning. *Ad fontes* is always in the foreground of Erasmus' thought.

From his historical critical approach Erasmus deduced certain facts that, though not always accepted in his day as valid, sound strikingly modern. He said that the Gospel of Matthew was probably originally written in Hebrew rather than Greek [16]; the Gospel of Mark was an abridgment of the Gospel of Matthew [17]. Erasmus thought that Luke was not an eyewitness to the events that he wrote about in his Gospel [18]. He also thought that the Epistle to the Hebrews was not written by Paul, though his argument for

---

15) "Apologia", Holborn, 166.4. "Nos in prima recognitione quattuor Graecis adiuti sumus, in secunda quinque, in tertia praeter alia accessit editio Asculana, in quarta praesto fuit et Hispaniensis, deinde consultis tum pervetustis tum emendatis aliquot Latinae linguae voluminibus."

16) LB ix, *Des. Erasmi Apologia in Dialogvm Jac. Latomi* I, 86 f. "Iam an Euangelium Matthaei primum sit Hebraice conscriptum, non est hujus argumenti differere: ... quanquam haud nesciam, id locis aliquot dicere Hieronymum, ... cum in Matthaeo multa sint loca, in quibus archetypi desiderabitur auctoritas, praesertim cum putet, alicubi in Graecorum codicibus nonnihil omissum, alicubi nonnihil additum ... Ac Hieronymus alicubi scribit, Euangelium, quod Matthaei titulo legitur a Nazareis, ipsis archetypam videri."
Cf. ibid., *Des. Erasmi Apologia ad Jac. Stvnicam*, 288 c. "Aliquoties admonueram, mihi non videri Matthaeum Euangelium suum scripsisse Hebraice, aut si scripsit, ab Hieronymo non fuisse visum. Id non assevero quidem, sed ajo, mihi videri probabilius."

17) LB vi, 151 e. "Et hic Hebraeorum more exorsus est ab ipsa operis titulo, quemadmodum Matthaeas, cuius epitomen scripsit Marcus, auctore Augustino."
Cf. ibid., 217 c. "Porro Marci Evangelium eius, quod a Matthaeo proditum est, videri possit epitome, multa praetermittens, et historiam Evangelicam auspicans a praedicatione Ioannis."

18) Ibid., 218 d. "Lucam non vidisse quae scribit in hoc libro."

this was supplemented by his grammatical criticism. In writing to Cardinal Matthew Skinner in the preface to the *Paraphrase on the Epistle of James*, he states, "By many arguments one may conjecture that the Epistle to Hebrews is not Paul's for it was written in rhetorical style rather than apostolic style" [19].

Although not always correct in these deductions, Erasmus nevertheless precurses the modern historical critical approach. If one considers the limited material that was available to him, one sees that Erasmus made great strides in utilizing an historical critical approach.

Erasmus wanted the Bible understood in its natural or historical sense. This, of course, was not different from his day [20], but to understand the literal meaning of the Scripture gives impetus to a utilization of a better historical critical approach. It is always this better understanding of the text that motivates Erasmus.

This historical critical method of Erasmus also flows over into the historical criticism of the Canon. It was a natural process for him to move from historical evaluation of the sources directly to an evaluation of their worth.

However, Erasmus' observations are based primarily on style, for his criterion was the historical document itself (he remains always the philologist). Of course, Erasmus was helped in his efforts to evaluate the Canon by the literature that became available because of the Renaissance interest in antiquity. Up until this period Augustine's *De doctrina Christiana* was the primary source of knowledge concerning the history of the Canon [21]. But Erasmus

---

19) Allen, 1171.6. "Siquidem quae fertur ad Hebraeas, praeterquam quod multis argumentis coniici potest non esse Pauli, cum stilo rhetorico verius quam Apostolico sit scripta."
Cf. LB ix, 27. "Apud me certe non constat hanc epistolam a Paulo scriptam Hebraice, etiamsi plerique id opinentur."

20) Erasmus' historical or literal approach is only a variation of the Scholastic concept of the *sensus litteralis* or *sensus historicus*.

21) *De doctrina Christiana*, 212 (8). "In canonicis autem scripturis ecclesiarum catholicarum quamplurium auctoritatem sequatur, inter quas sane illae sint, quae apostolicas sedes habere et epistolas accipere meruerunt. Tenebit igitur hunc modum in scripturis canonicis, ut eas, quae ab omnibus accipiuntur ecclesiis catholicis, praeponat eis, quas quaedam non accipiunt: in eis vero, quae non accipiuntur ab omnibus, praeponat eas, quas plures gravioresque accipiunt, eis quas pauciores minorisque auctoritatis ecclesiae tenent. Si autem alias invenerit a pluribus, alias a gravioribus haberi, quam-

had available Eusebius' and Jerome's [22] accounts of the doubtful settlement of the Canon, together with other heretofore little known writings of the Fathers, which he naturally utilized to arrive at his conclusions.

The Middle Age position on the authority of the Canon was that it was authoritative because it had been handed down from the ancient church as authoritative. The form of the New Testament Canon was the same as in the sixth century, and there was no real question as to its authority. The position was one of defense rather than questioning. This period did not contribute anything new to the Canon dispute of the earlier centuries nor did it even consider the problem that at one time some of the books in the New Testament had been contested.

Thomas of Aquinas had stated the Middle Age position on the Canon when he said that the authority of the canonical Scriptures is used exclusively from the necessity of argument, while the authority of the doctors of the Church argue from probability. "For our faith rests upon the revelation of the Apostles and Prophets who wrote the canonical books" [23]. And in another place Thomas

---

quam hoc facile invenire non possit, aequalis tamen auctoritatis eas habendas puto."

Ibid., 213. "His quadraginta quatuor libris Testamenti Veteris terminatur auctoritas. Novi autem quatuor libris evangelii, secundum Matthaeum, secundum Marcum, secundum Lucam, secundum Ioannem, quatuordecim epistolis Pauli apostoli, ad Romanos, ad Corinthios duabus, ad Galatas, ad Ephesios, ad Philippenses, ad Thessalonicenses duabus, ad Colossenses, ad Timotheum duabus, ad Titum, ad Philemonem, ad Hebraeos, Petri duabus, tribus Iohannis, una Iudae et una Iacobi, actibus apostolorum libro uno et apocalypsi Iohannis libro uno."

22) De vir inlustr. 5. "(Paulus) scripsit autem novem ad septem ecclesias epistulas: ad Romanos unam, ad Corinthios duas, ad Galatas unam, ad Ephesios unam, ad Philippenses unam, ad Colossenses unam, ad Thessalonicenses duas; praeterea ad discipulos suos, Timotheo duas, Tito unam, Philemoni unam. Epistula autem quae fertur ad Hebraeos non eius creditur propter stili sermonisque dissonantiam, sed vel Barnabae iuxta Tertullianum, vel Lucae evangelistae iuxta quosdam, vel Clementis, Romanae postea ecclesiae episcopi, quem aiunt sententias Pauli proprio ordinasse et ornasse sermone, vel certe, quia Paulus scribebat ad Hebraeos et propter invidiam sui apud eos nominis titulum in principio salutationis amputaverat (scripserat autem ut Hebraeus Hebraice, id est, suo eloquio disertissime) ea quae eloquenter scripta fuerant in Hebraeo, eloquentius vertisse in Graecum et hanc esse causam, quod a ceteris Pauli epistulis discrepare videatur."

23) Summa Theol. I q. 1, a. 8. "Autoritatibus autem canonicae scripturae vtitur proprie ex necessitate argumentando. Autoritatibus autem aliorum

says, "For Holy Scripture is the rule of faith and it is neither allowed to be added to nor subtracted from" [24].

Johannes Leipoldt, in his work on the New Testament Canon, says of the Middle Age position on the authority of the Canon, "Der neutestamentliche Kanon galt als Authorität, weil man ihn von alten Kirchen als Authorität empfangen hatte, also weil er das wichtigste Stück der kirchlichen Überlieferung war" [25]. It was just this type of thinking that the humanistically oriented mind of Erasmus was opposed to, and with his principle of *ad fontes* Erasmus was delighted to have an opportunity to challenge such a concept of authority as the Middle Ages presented.

Erasmus was very interested in the seven New Testament *antilegomena:* Hebrews, James, Second Peter, Second and Third John, and Revelation [26]. To examine its worth compelled his attention because it gave him an opportunity to reveal his scholarship and knowledge of the subject. But it also gave him an opportunity to bring the writings of the ancients to light, and at the same time provided an opportunity to challenge the typical Scholastic thinking on the subject. The seven *antilegomena* played such an important part in his thinking on authenticity that late in life he wrote that the primary works of the New Testament were the four Gospels, the Acts of the Apostles, the Pauline Epistles (except that written to the Hebrews), I Peter, and I John [27].

---

doctorum ecclesiae, quasi arguendo ex propriis, sed probabiliter. Innititur enim fides nostra revelationi Apostolis, et Prophetis factae, qui canonicos libros scripserunt."

24) Ibid., II/II q. 1, a. 9. "Sacra enim Scriptura est regulai fidei, cui nec addere, nec subtrahere licet."

25) *Geschichte des neutestamentlichen Kanons,* Band 2, p. 4.

26) Allen, 1171.1, to Matthew Skinner (preface to Epistle of James). "Iam videbar ad huius curriculi metam peruenisse, et ipse mihi ferias destinabam in hoc duntaxat genere studiorum, propterea quod omnes Epistolas explicuissem quas Pauli germanas esse iudicabam; quibus adiunxi Petri duas et Iudac vnam, quod hae non solum consentirent cum Paulinis in vigore doctrinae Euangelicae, verum maioribus etiam tenebris quam illae essent inuolutae. Siquidem quae fertur ad Hebraeos, praeterquam quod multis argumentis coniici potest non esse Pauli, cum stilo rhetorico verius quam Apostolico sit scripta, non perinde multam habet difficultatis: quemadmodum nec eae quae Iacobo Ioannique tribuntur. Nam Ioannis ipsa sermonis copia veluti sui ipsius interpres est, et Iacobus fere versatur in locis communibus."

27) LB v, 1049 f, *Ecclesiastae III.* "Novi vero sunt hi, quatuor Euangelia, Acta Apostolorum, Pauli Epistolae omnes, excepta ea quae scribuntur ad

In order to understand the significance of Erasmus' place in the history of the Canon it is necessary to illustrate briefly the positions that were held by earlier writers such as Jerome, and Augustine, and the Middle Age view as held by Thomas of Aquinas and Nicholas of Lyra. The Epistle to the Hebrews, because of its length and theological importance, exemplifies these various positions on the authenticity and canononical value of this writing.

Because he had little knowledge of Greek, Augustine was hazy and uncertain concerning the history of the Greek church and its Canon development. Accordingly, his position on the authorship of the Epistle to the Hebrews is not entirely clear [28]. Yet Augustine seems to arrive at the conviction that the Epistle is an authentic Pauline Epistle and therefore it should be included in the Canon, for in *De doctrina Christiana* he closes his list of the canonical writings of Paul with the Epistle to the Hebrews [29].

Jerome, when discussing the epistles of Paul, lists epistles to seven churches: Romans, Corinthians (2), Galatians, Ephesians, Philippians, Colossians and Thessalonians (2). In addition to these, Jerome says that Paul wrote letters to his disciples: Timothy (2), Titus (1), and Philemon (1). Then he discusses the Epistle to the Hebrews through the use of valued earlier Fathers. Tertullian held the letter to be written by Barnabas, while others regarded it as coming from the hand of Luke or from Clement of Rome, or perhaps the letter is Pauline, but grounded on a Hebrew original [30]. However, in his letters Jerome is not so clear, leaning at times away from Pauline authorship, at other times leaning toward it [31].

Hebraeos, prima Petri, et prima Ioannis. Non quod caeteris adimam auctoritatem, sed quod horum praecipua sit auctoritas."
Cf. Erasmus' Old Testament Canon (ibid., 1049 f.). "Cuius ordinis sunt Genesis, Exodus, Leviticus, Numeri, Deuteronomium, Josuae, Judicum, Ruth, Regorum quatuor, Paralipomenon duo, totidem Esdrae, Hester, Job, Psalmi, Esaias, Hieromias, Ezechiel, Daniel, Prophetae duodecim."
See LB ix, 747 c. (*Des. Erasmi Apologia Adversus Debacchationes Sutoris*) where Erasmus gives the historical facts concerning the Antilogomena (cf. LB ix, 866 c ff. *Des. Erasmi Declarationes ad censuru facultatis theologiae Parismesis*).
28) *De civitate Dei* 16.22. "... in epistola, quae inscribitur ad Hebraeos, quam plures Pauli apostoli esse dicunt, quidam vero negant ..."
29) See footnote 21.
30) See footnote 22.
31) Epistle 129.3. to Dardanus. "Illud nostris dicendum est, hanc epistolam quae inscribitur ad Hebraeos non solum ab ecclesiis orientis, sed ab

As Johannes Leipoldt observed, "Er wollte auf diese Weise gegen-über beiden Parteien, Griechen und Lateinern, decken"[32].

In his preface to the exposition of the Epistle to the Hebrew, Thomas Aquinas defended the Pauline authorship of Hebrews, knowing that before the Council of Nicaea its authenticity was disputed and that its position in the Canon was doubted. But he was under the impression that after the Council of Nicaea this was no longer the case. He puts forward the arguments against Pauline authorship, such as the method and style not being the same as the other epistles, the author being perhaps the evangelist Luke or Barnabas or Clement of Rome. He also included the argument that Paul had stated in Galatians 2.8 that Peter was appointed apostle to the Jews but he was appointed apostle to the nations. Another argument is that the name of Paul was hated by the Jews, as told in his conversion experience in Acts, chapter 12, and that the Epistle was probably originally written in Hebrew since it is ad-dressed to Jews. Thomas refutes these arguments against Pauline authenticity by stating that many antique doctors accepted this Epistle as the testimony of Paul. In countering the other arguments he quotes scripture to show that Paul could write in all languages and styles (I Corinthians 14.8) and he ends with the statement that Luke could have translated the epistle into Greek from the He-brew[33].

After reading Thomas' statements defending the authenticity of the Pauline authorship of the Epistle to the Hebrews, one can understand why Erasmus wrote of this that Thomas did such a

---

omnibus retro ecclesiasticis Graeci sermonis scriptoribus quasi Pauli apostoli suscipi, licet plerique eam vel Barnabae vel Clementis arbitrentur, et nihil interesse, cuius sit, cum ecclesiastici viri sit et cotidie ecclesiarum lectione celebretur. Quodsi eam Latinorum consuetudo non recipit inter scripturas canonicas, nec Graecorum quidem ecclesiae apocalypsem Ioannis eadem liber-tate suscipiunt; et tamen nos utramque suscipimus nequaquam huius temporis consuetudinem, sed veterum scriptorum auctoritatem sequentes, qui plerum-que utriusque abutuntur testimoniis, non ut interdum de apocryphis facere solent, quippe qui et gentilium litterarum raro utantur exemplis, sed quasi canonicis et ecclesiasticis."

Cf. Epistles 53.8. "... ad Paulinum: Paulus apostolus ad septem ecclesias scribit; octava enim ad Hebraeos a plerisque numerum ponitur, ..."

32) Leipoldt, op. cit., I, p. 229.

33) Preface to the exposition of Hebrews. "Sciendum est, quod ante synodum Nicaenam quidam dubitaverunt, an ista epistola esset Pauli. Et quod non, probant duobus argumentis. Unum est, quia non tenet hunc

poor job of defending the Pauline authorship, that he would have done better if he had never attempted a defense of it [34].

Nicholas of Lyra, like Thomas, and for that matter all the Middle Age interpreters, considered the Epistle to the Hebrews as a canonical and authentic Pauline Epistle. His critical remarks on the authorship of this Epistle come close to being a treatise on the subject. But in his lengthy attempt to prove Pauline authorship, Nicholas actually does more to undermine what he is attempting than to affirm it. In his prologue to the Epistle to the Hebrews, he begins his explanation in much the same vein as Thomas. In fact, he seems to have the text of Thomas open to that very page. After stating more or less the same type of arguments that Thomas pursues as to why some felt it was not an authentic letter of Paul, Nicholas then moves to what we can term "the Catholic position" on the question. It is here that the real distinction from the development of Thomas is seen. First, Nicholas says the Epistle is authentic because the *authority of the Church* at the council of Nicaea determined it to be written by the Apostle; second, (note the authority of the

---

modum, quem in aliis epistolis. Non enim praemittit hic salutationem nec nomen suum. Aliud est, quia non sapit stylum aliarum, immo habet elegantiorem; nec est aliqua scriptura, quae sic ornate procedat in ordine verborum et in sententiis sicut ista. Unde dicebant ipsam esse vel Lucae evangelistae vel Barnabae vel Clementis papae; ipse enim scripsit Atheniensibus quasi per omnia secundum stylum istum. Sed antiqui doctores, praecipue Dionysius et alii aliqui, accipiunt verba huius epistolae pro testimoniis Pauli. Et Hieronymus illam inter epistolas Pauli recipit. Ad primum ergo dicendum est, quod triplex ratio fuit, quare non posuit nomen suum. Una est, quia non erat apostolus Iudaeorum, sed gentium. Galat. ii, 8 ... Et ideo non fecit mentionem de apostolatu suo in principio huius epistolae, quia nolebat officium sui apostolatus insinuare nisi ipsis gentibus. Secunda, quia nomen suum Iudaeis erat odiosum, cum diceret, legalia non debere servari, ut patet Act. xxii, et ideo ipsum tacuit, ne saluberrima doctrina huius epistolae abiiceretur. Tertia, quia Iudaeus erat: ii. Cor. xi 22 ... Et domestici non bene sustinent excellentiam suorum: Matth. xiii 57 ... Ad argumentum secundum dicendum est, quod ideo est elegantior in stylo, quia, etsi sciebat omnem linguam: i. Corinth. xiv 18 ..., tamen melius sciebat Hebraeam tamquam sibi magis connaturalem, in qua scripsit epistolam istam. Et ideo magis ornate potuit loqui in idiomate suo quam in aliquo alio. Unde dicit ii. Corinth. xi 6 ... Lucas autem, qui fuit optimus prolocutor, istum ornatum transtulit de Hebraeo in Graecum."

34) LB ix, 866. "... solvit ille quidem dubitantium argumenta, sed adeo frigide, ut satius fuerit non attigisse. Nec illa tamen erant praecipua dubitandi argumenta, nomen praetermissum ac stylus nonnihil varians. Erant alia non pauca aliquanto graviora, quae movebant eruditos."

Fathers) Dionysius the disciple of Paul, states that it is authentic; third, the argument of Chrysostum; fourth, the authorship is clear in the last chapter of this epistle, where it is evidenced by the reference to Timothy, who was the spiritual brother of Paul; fifth, the zeal of Paul for the Jews was attested in Romans, chapter 9; sixth, the zeal of Paul toward the proclaiming of evangelical truth as seen in the second chapter of Galatians [35].

Erasmus was not only well aware of the ancient writings on the history of the Canon, as we have mentioned, but he also knew the accounts of Thomas and Nicholas. Since he was at the same time grounded in the humanistic concept of questioning the accepted modes, such as the medieval acceptance of the Canon verbatim, he read these accounts with interest and, in the case of the Scholastic expositions and explanations, with critical eyes.

In his remarks on Hebrews 13.24, Erasmus begins by stating that the Epistle should not be less cherished just because the authorship is doubtful. Whoever the author is, the Epistle is worth reading by

---

35) Prologue to the *Postilla fratis Nicolai de Lira super epistolas Pauli ad Hebraeos.* "Ad maiorem autem sequentium et praedictorum evidentiam quaeritur, utrum haec epistola sit Pauli apostoli. Et arguitur primo quod non, quia in hac epistola non tenetur modus scribendi, qui est in aliis epistolis Pauli, praeponendo nomen suum et sui apostolatus officium, ut patet; ergo etc. Item quia elegantior est stilus in hac epistola quam in aliis. Ad contrarium est usus et consuetudo ecclesiae, in qua allegatur ista epistola tanquam ab apostolo scripta. Respondeo dicendo quod propter rationes praedictas ab aliquibus fuit opinatum, quod haec epistola non esset Pauli; propter quod aliqui dicebant, quod erat epistola Clementis papae et martiris; et movebantur ad hoc, quia ipse scripsit Atheniensibus epistolam per omnia consimilem. Alii autem dicebant quod erat Lucae evangelistae et movebantur ad hoc quia ipse eam primo scripsit Graece, ut dicitur in prologo. Alii autem dicebant quod erat Terculiani, qui fuit propinquus apostolorum tempori. Sed modo indubitanter tenetur quod est epistola Pauli, quod probatur multiplici ratione. Primo auctoritate ecclesiae, cuius est talia dubia determinare; in sinodo autem Nicaeno recepit ecclesia istam epistolam tanquam ab apostolo scriptam. Secundo hoc idem probatur per auctoritatem antiquorum doctorum et potissime beati Dionisii, qui fuit discipulus beati Pauli. Iste autem in scriptis suis allegat dicta huius epistolae tanquam dicta Pauli magistri sui. Tertio hoc probatur ex auctoritate Crisostomi super epistolam istam dicentis quod Paulus eam scripsit Romae existens. Postquam enim biennio Romae fuerat propter appellationem factam ad Caesarem, de qua habetur in actibus apostolorum, habuit licentiam transeundi in Hispaniam; et Iudaeos ibi vidit; et postea Romam rediens de illo loco hanc epistolam eis scripsit, ut dicit Crisostimus. Quarto patet propositum ex his quae dicuntur ultimo capitulo huius epistolae,

Christians. And as to Paul's style there had been far and wide disagreement, nevertheless the letter approaches the spirit and heart of Paul. There are certain arguments that make it impossible for Paul to be the author. First, Paul's name is not prefixed. Then, Jerome testified in his letters that it was of questionable authorship. In this connection Ambrose, who wrote a commentary on all the Pauline epistles, did not write one on the Epistle to the Hebrews. Moreover certain passages favor heretical doctrines. Here Erasmus is referring to the ancient controversy over Hebrews 6.4 ff., which he says contradicts the receiving back of the lapsed into the communion of the Saints as Paul has stated in I Corinthians 5.1 ff. (cf. II Corinthians 2.8), all of which is part of the argument on the problem of forgiveness of sins after baptism. But the most certain argument is the style itself and the character of the discourse, which bear no affinity to the writings of Paul. As to the argument that Paul wrote in Hebrew and Luke kept the contents of the epistle in his memory and reproduced it in his own style, Ersamus does not care to comment. It is not the words alone, nor the form, that are in disagreement, but the entire letter is at variance with the writings of Paul. It is probable, as Jerome has indicated in *Catalogo Scriptorum illustrium*, that the author is Clement, pontifex of Rome, the fourth Peter [36].

---

videlicet quod missa fuit haec epistola per Thimotheum, qui fuit filius spiritualis Pauli apostoli. Quinto hoc idem arguitur ex zelo apostoli ad salutem Iudaeorum: de quo zelo dicit ad Ro. ix: Optabam anathema esse pro fratribus meis qui sunt dogmati mei ex quibus Christus secundum carnem. Ad Ro. xi: Quamdiu sum apostolus gentium, ministerium meum honorificabo, si quos provocem ad aemulandum carnem meam, id est Iudaeos ut salvum faciam aliquos ex eis. Ideo non est aliquid modo probabile, quoniam Paulus scripsit Iudaeis ad eorum salutem, qui tot alia scripsit aliis gentibus pro salute earundem? Nulla autem alia epistola Pauli dicitur scripta Hebraeis nisi ista; ergo, etc. Sexto probatur propositum ex zelo Pauli apostoli ad evangelicam veritatem; ex quo zelo reprehendit Petrum manifeste, ut habetur ad Gal. ii."

36) LB vi, 1023. *Annotationes ad Hebraeos* 13.24. "Optime lector, nihilo minoris velim esse tibi hanc Epistolam, quod a multis dubitatum sit Pauli esset, an alterius. Certe cuiuscunque est, multis nominibus digna est, quae legatur a Christianis. Et ut a stilo Pauli, quod ad phrasim attinet, longe lateque discrepat: ita ad spiritum ac pectus Paulinum vehementer accedit. Verum ut non potest doceri certis argumentis cuius sit, quod nullius habeat inscriptionem, ita compluribus indiciis colligi potest, ab alio quopiam quam a Paulo scriptam fuisse. Primum quod sola omnium Pauli nomen non praeferat, Tametsi non me fugit hoc utcunque dilui ab Hieronymo ... Deinde

The Epistle of Jude was not above Erasmus' suspicion because it borrows from a Hebrew apocalyptic work[37]. Second and third John were probably the work of John the presbyter, rather than the writing of the evangelist John. Working from the remark of Jerome[38], Erasmus states that the apostle John wrote the fourth Gospel and the first Epistle of John, but that the last two Epistles of John were written by the presbyter John, not John the Apostle[39].

---

quod tot annis, nempe usque ad aetatem Hieronymi non recepta fuerit a Latinis, quemadmodum ipse testatur in epistolis suis. Ad hanc conjecturam facit, quod Ambrosius, cum omnes Paulinas epistolas sit interpretatus, in hanc unam nihil scripserit. Vt ne dicam interim inesse locos aliquot, qui quorumdam haereticorum dogmatibus patrocinari videantur. Velut illa, quod velum separans sancta sanctorum, interpretatur coelum, ac multo magis, quod palam adimere videatur spema baptismo relapsis in peccatum, idque non uno in loco, cum Paulus et eum receperit in communionem sanctorum, qui dormierat cum uxore patris. Adde huc, quod diuus Hieronymus cum aliis aliquot locis ita citat huius epistolae testimonia, ut de autore uideatur ambigere, tum edisserens caput Hieremiae tricesimum primum, hoc, inquit, testimonio Paulus apostolus, sive quis alius scripsit epistolam, usus est ad Hebraeos ... Restat iam argumentum illud, quo non aliud certius, stilus ipse, et orationis, qui nihil habet affinitatis cum phrasi Paulina. Nam quod adferunt hic quidam Paulum ipsum hebraice scripsisse, caeterum Lucam argumentum epistolae, quam memoria tenebat suis explicuisse verbis quantum valeat, viderint alii. Neque enim in uerbis solum aut figuris discrimen est, sed omnibus notis dissidet. Et ut Paulus graece scribens, multum ex idiomate sermonis hebraici retulit, ita et in hac quam ut uolunt isti, scripsit hebraice, nonnulla sermonis illius vestigia resideret. Quid quod ne Lucas quidem ipse, in actis apostolorum, hoc est, in argumento, quod facile recipit orationis ornamenta, parum abest ab huius epistolae eloquentia. Equidem haud interponam hoc loco meam sententiam. Caeterum admodum probabile est, quod indicauit diuus Hieronymus in catalogo scriptorum illustrium, Clementem Rhomanum pontificem, a Petro quartum, autorem huius epistolae fuisse."

37) LB vi, 1090. "Porro locus quem hic citat Iudas sumptus est ex apocryphis Hebraeorum unde et ipsa epistola non caruit suspicione."
Cf., Jerome, *de vir inlustr.* 9 (Jude) "... parvam quae de septem catholicis est epistulam reliquit, et quia de libro Enoch, qui apocryphus est, in ea adsumit testimonium, a plerisque reicitur; tamen auctoritatem vetustate iam et usu meruit, et inter sanctas scripturas conputatur."

38) Ibid., (John) "... scripsit autem et unam epistulam cuius exordium est 'Quod fuit ab initio, quod audivimus et vidimus oculis nostris, quod perspeximus et manus nostrae temptaverunt de verbo vitae', quae ab universis ecclesiasticis et eruditis viris probatur. Reliquae autem duae quarum principium est 'Senior electae dominae et natis eius' et sequentis 'Senior Gaio carissimo, quem ego diligo in veritate' Iohannis presbyteri adseruntur, cuius et hodie alterum sepulcrum apud Ephesum ostenditur et nonnulli putant duas memorias eiusdem, Iohannis evangelistae esse."

Erasmus saw no manuscripts that attributed the Epistle James to the Apostle James. The ancient Church had not known who the writer was. The letter does not contain any of the Hebraic expressions that would be natural to James the Just, primate of Jerusalem. Erasmus accepts the Epistle although he thinks that it does not possess apostolic weight and majesty [40].

The Second Epistle of Peter is also controversial. Erasmus himself fluctuated on the authorship, just as Jerome before him [41]. Erasmus knew that the ancient Church had argued over the authenticity of this work and he knew also that the style of the book was quite different from the First Epistle of Peter. He felt as well that this letter did not correspond in apostolic majesty to the first epistle. At one time Erasmus admits the possibility that Second Peter was a falsification. He states that because the authorship of the Epistle is in doubt, anyone who wished to could have written this letter and set forth his own thinking as that of Peter [42].

---

39) LB vi, 1088 c (3 John 3.12). "Constat inter Auctores, primam Ioannis Epistolam eius esse Ioannis, quem Jesus dilexit plurimum. Caeterum duas posteriores Ioannes Presbyter scripsit, non Ioannes Apostolus."
Cf., LB ix, 867 d. "Qui hoc opus negebant esse Ioannis evangelistae, aut alium fuisse Ioannem ab evangelista credebant, quemadmodum duas posteriores epistolas adscribebant Ioanni non evangelistae sed presbytero."

40) LB vi, 1038 d (James 5.20). "Nec enim referre videtur usquequaque majestatem illam et gravitatem Apostolorum. Nec Hebraismi tantum, quantum a Iacobo, qui fuerit Episcopus Hierosolymitanus, exspectaretur. Divus Hieronymus in Catalogo Scriptorum illustrium ex auctoritate Hegesippi indicat multos huius nominis fuisse Discipulos. Et, ipse in titulo Epistolae non appellat sese Apostolum, quanquam in nostris adjectum est Apostoli cognomen, sed reclamantibus magno consensu Graecorum exemplaribus."
Ibid., 1025 b (James 1.1). "Iacobus Apostolus, Apostolos non additur in his libris, quos ego viderim, nec in Latinis emendatioribus."

41) De vir inlustr. 9. (Simon Peter) "... scripsit duas epistulas, quae catholicae nominantur, quarum secunda a plerisque eius negatur, propter stili cum priore dissonantiam."

42) LB vi, 1061 d (2 Peter 1.17). "Quum hic profiteatur se fuisse unum, qui in monte audiere transfigurato Domino Patris vocem, mirum est aliquos dubitasse an haec Epistola esse Petri."
Cf. ibid., 1068 c (2 Peter 3.17). "De hac quoque secunda Petri Epistola, cuius esse, controversia erat. Id testatur Hieronymus in Catalogo Scripturum illustrium ... At idem alias variat, nunc volens eam esse Petri, et stili dissonantiam rejiciens in interpretem, quo tum Petrus sit usus: nunc negans illius esse, quod reclamet stilus."
Cf. LB ix, 866 f. "Qui de auctore secundae Petri dubitabant, non erant tam stupidi, quin viderent illic fieri mentionem de visione montis; sed suspica-

But of all the seven *antilegomena* the book of Revelation was to catch the brunt of Erasmus' criticism. He said that there were many learned men who argue and dispute the writings as being of a fraudulent nature, saying that it does not have any apostolic value and that it encloses the historical figures of the time. The thoughts themselves, they say, have nothing which is worthy of the apostolic majesty, even though, Erasmus adds, the style has a resemblance to the Gospel of John and the Epistle of John. Apart from these critics Erasmus noticed that the author, in writing this work, went to a great deal of trouble to include his name, "I, John; I, John", whereas the evangelist John concealed his name and person. Furthermore, in the Greek codices "the evangelist John" is not written, but rather the words, "John the presbyter". In one place Erasmus states that if one denies that Revelation is written by the Evangelist John, he must either see another John as the author or he must hold the book to be a falsification [43]. Erasmus' conclusion is a compromise:

> "If the agreement of the entire world did not call me to other thoughts, particularly the authority of the Church, I would not consider this writing to be from the pen of John the evangelist, and therefore possess full canonical authority, and on a level with the other canonical writings. When I observe the malice of heretics, I am near the thought that Gerinth, who lived in the time of John, and that, I am of the opinion, survived him, composed this, wishing to pour out his poison on the world. But I cannot persuade myself that God could have permitted this ruse of the devil during all these centuries of Christian people. This book is not worth the discussion of it, for it contains only allegories, although it is of great interest for a knowledge of the Church" [44].

bantur illam epistolam scriptam abs quopiam, qui cupiebat illam legi sub nomine Petri. Id quo facilius persuaderet, addidisse mentionem de visione. Eam vero suspicionem conceperant ex phrasi, eque pectore ac vigore sententiarum, quae partim videbantur ad imitationem alterius epistolae effictae, partim non perinde respondentes apostolici ordinis principis majestati."

43) LB ix, 867 c. "Qui hoc opus negabant esse Ioannis evangelistae, aut alium fuisse Ioannem ab evangelista credebant, quemadmodum duas posteriores epistolas adscribebant Ioanni, non evangelistae sed presbytero: aut eum qui conscripsit librum, id egisse, ut ab evangelista scriptus videretur eoque locum suo instituto commodum affinxisse. Si quis hoc commentum clamet absurdum, patiar hic absurdissimum videri, modo sciat illo saeculo mundum fuisse differtum libris apocryphis alienum titulum praeferentibus. Idque pii quoque homines sibi persuaserant non tantum licere, verum etiam officiosum esse."

44) LB vi, 1123 c. "Ad haec quosdam eruditissimos viros totum hoc argumentum ceu fictum multis convitiis insectatos fuisse, quasi nihil haberet

Erasmus made several other observations of authorship of the New Testament Epistles outside of the *antilegomena*. These are especially interesting as they point up his historical critical approach in itself, rather than having as a basis opinions previously written on the history of the canon.

On the Epistle to the Ephesians Erasmus noted in his remark to chapter 1.1 that

"In this epistle one discovers all the fervor of Paul, all the profundity of Paul, also all of his spirit and heart, but there is no other place where his style is so annoyingly troublesome and so filled with figures of speech of all kind, whether this is the fault of the interpreter which he used or that the words could not attain the height of his thoughts" [45].

Erasmus states that the first Epistle of Peter was written in Babylon.

"I would prefer to believe that Peter lived for a time in Babylon ... it is a frivolous argument to pretend that the primate of the apostolic seat was disturbed if Peter wrote this epistle in Babylon" [46].

Apostolicae gravitatis, sed vulgatam tantum rerum historiam figurarum involucris adumbratam. Deinde, nec in sententiis esse quod Apostolica majestate dignum videatur. Ut de his interim nihil dicam, me nonnihil moverent cum aliae conjecturae, tum illae, quod revelationes scribens, tam sollicite suum inculcat nomen, ego Ioannes, ego Ioannes ... Ut ne commemorem stilum non parum dissonantem ab eo qui est in Evangelio et Epistola ... Haec, inquam, me non nihil moverent, quominus crederem esse Joannis Evangelistae, nisi me consensus orbis alio vocaret, praecipue vero auctoritas Ecclesiae, si tamen hoc opus hoc animo comprobat Ecclesia, ut Ioannis Evangelistae velit haberi, et pari esse pondere cum caeteris canonicis libris ... (1527): Equidem quum ad Haereticorum malitiosas artes respicio, facile possum adduci ut credam Cerinthum qui vixit aetate Ioannis, et illi, opinor, supervixit, hoc commento voluisse suum virus in orbem spargere. At rursum mihi non potest persuaderi Deum passurum fuisse, ut Diaboli techna tot saeculis impune deluderet populum Christianum ... Ad evincendum hic liber non perinde valet, quum totus constet allegoriis, ad cognoscenda Ecclesiae primordia conducit plurimum. (1527)."

45) Ibid., 831. "Ad Eph. 1.1: Idem in hac Epistola Pauli fervor, eadem profonditas, idem omnino spiritus ac pectus: verum non alibi sermo hyperbatis, aliisque incommoditatibus molestior, sive id interpretis fuit, quo fuit usus in hac, sive sensuum sublimitatem sermonis facultas non est assequuta."

46) Ibid., 1056. I Peter 5.13: "Magis arbitror Petrum Babylone id temporis vere vixisse ...: Frivolum vero est, quod quidam cavillantur, vacillare principatum Romanae sedis, si Petrus hanc Epistolam scripsit Babylone."

The Epistle to Philemon is definitely the work of Paul:

> "I am astonished that one could doubt that this epistle is from Saint Paul, for nothing could be more Pauline than the account and method of argument of this letter" [47].

Erasmus played an important and decisive role in the history of the New Testament Canon [48]. As we have seen, Erasmus not only had a firm grasp of the history of the Canon, but he enlarged upon these facts, particularly in his *Annotationes* to the New Testament. These remarks and judgments were widely read since this was the first critical work on the New Testament to appear. The influence that Erasmus was able to generate is difficult to measure, but the impact of his statements must have had a considerable effect. The value of Erasmus' thought was in his elaboration on the historical facts, both the positive and critical side of the history of the Canon, perhaps even more so than in his concepts of the authenticity of the canonical writings. This exposition of the facts behind the development of the Canon was to bring a new world of material into the hands of men who would have no other means of obtaining these historical facts, for although the writings of the ancients had been rediscovered, they were not as yet available to all who wished them.

There are several conclusions we can draw from Erasmus' critical approach to the Canon. First, he felt that the authority of the Scripture was in no way challenged by a dispute as to apostolic authorship of the canonical writings. Provided the whole of the facts on which our salvation rests are established, then there is no worry over a slight variance in word or thought or style. He remarked on the Epistle to the Hebrews that one should not discard nor disdain this writing just because the Pauline authorship was contested [49].

---

47) Ibid., 980. "Quo magis etiam admiror ullos de hac epistola dubitasse, num Pauli esset, cum pro ratione modoque argumenti nihil esse magis Paulinum possit."

48) Leipoldt, op. cit., II, p. 13. "Der bedeutendste von ihnen (the humanists) war der grosse Desiderius Erasmus. Er stand auch in der Geschichte des neutestamentlichen Kanons an einem entscheidenden Wandelpunkte. Zwar hat er an den überlieferten Autoritäten nicht gerüttelt oder wenigstens nicht rütteln wollen. Aber er hat andere veranlasst, das zu tun."

49) See footnote 36.

Secondly, human errors of judgment and feeling do not damage the meaning and worth of the Scriptures, nor should the fact that the Apostles are ignorant of certain things disturb our faith. Only Christ possesses the truth, and he alone never makes an error. Therefore, our faith should not be less if there is dispute over the Canon, but more because of Christ [50]. Here we see again the theme of the *philosophia Christi* which runs throughout Erasmus' writings.

Thirdly, the Scriptures contain our best knowledge of the original Church, even if the authorship is disputable, and therefore have great value. The fact that Erasmus could make this statement when talking of the book of Revelation, which he felt was the least of the New Testament books in value, points out his firm belief in this principle [51].

There is a marked development or perhaps deterioration, according to the way one approaches it, in Erasmus' use of the historical critical method, particularly in his statements concerning the Canon. This is without doubt caused by the pressure of the Roman church in her attempt to combat the powerful thrust of the Lutheran heresy. The demands of the Church upon her faithful were for an orthodoxy that had not been stressed to such a degree in several centuries. Erasmus felt this, and felt it deeply, with men such as John Eck, who attempted, even to the extreme of using devious means, to catch him in some form of heresy. The beginning of Erasmus' critical approach bears all the evidence of freedom, a humanistic, inquisitive freedom at that, but once the Reformation made itself known, then Erasmus assumes a cautious attitude, and even an orthodox one when under attack.

This last sentence is easily understandable when we examine Erasmus' struggle with the Sorbonne. In July, 1526, they censured

---

50) LB vi, 12. Matthew 2.6. "Neque enim continuo forte vacillet totius Scripturae Sacrae auctoritas, sicubi variant, vel in verbis, vel in sensu, modo summa constet earum rerum de quibus agitur, et unde cardo pendet nostrae salutis. Ut enim Spiritus ille divinus mentium Apostolicarum moderator, passus est suos ignorare quaedam, et labi errareque alicubi judicio sive affectu, non solum nullo incommodo Evangelii, sed hunc etiam ipsum errorem vertit in adjumentum nostrae fidei, ita fieri potuit, ut ita temperarit organum apostolicae memoriae, ut etiam si quid humano more fugisset, id non solum non deroget fidei divinae Scripturae, verum etiam fidem arroget ... *Solus Christus dictus est veritas, unus ille caruit omni errore.*"

51) See footnote 44.

Erasmus for his unorthodox views concerning the Canon. In ealier times, they said, the Church had contested the authorship of certain books, but now that was at an end. The Church had reached a decision and its decision was binding for all. They concluded by refuting his statements concerning the debated books one by one [52].

Erasmus was placed in a difficult position, which is quite an understatement if one considers the power of the Sorbonne theologians. Nevertheless, with his enormous tact he answered them. First, the author of the Holy Scriptures is the Holy Spirit, on this he is in full agreement with them. Moreover, all the writings are canonical and should remain so, even if he had expressed a critical appraisal of the authorship of the book. The names that appear in the preface to the books should remain as they are, without change,

---

52) LB ix, 863 ff. (*Underlined* statements are those of Erasmus). "*Non statim dubius est in fide, qui de auctore libri dubitat.* Haec propositio temerarie et errone asseritur, loquendo ut scriptor loquitur de dubio auctorum sacrorum librorum Novi Testamenti ab ecclesia sub nomine talium auctorum receptorum. Cuiusmodi sunt auctores quator librorum evangeliorum, septem epistolarum canonicarum, quatuordecim epistolarum Pauli, actuum apostolicorum et apocalypsis. Nam cum deus viros illos sanctos organa sua constituerit in editione talium librorum, honori eorum detrahit, quisquis ab huiusmodi libris nomina eorum aufert vel in dubium vertit, nec non et a frequenti abducit et fructuosa eorumdem lectione. Praeterea quamvis de auctoribus aliquorum huiusmodi librorum a nonnullis olim dubitatum sit, nihilominus, postquam ecclesia sub nomine talium auctorum suo usu universali illos recepit et sua probavit definitione, iam non fas est Christiano de illis dubitare aut in dubium revocare. *De epistolae ad Hebraeos auctore semper est dubitatum, et ipse, (ut ingenue fatear), adhuc dubito.* Hae duae propositiones arroganter et schismatice asseruntur contra usum et determinationem ecclesiae in multis conciliis, Nicaeno, Laudicensi, Carthaginensi tertio, cui adfuit Augustinus, et in concilio septuaginta episcoporum praeside Gelasio. Hoc insuper liquet, quia auctor huius epistolae dicit illam se misisse per Timotheum fratrem suum; suius legatione in quibusdam aliis epistolis solebat uti Paulus. Idem etiam demonstrat beatus Petrus, qui in fine secundae canonicae ad Hebraeos destinatae, quibus et primam miserat, eisdem dicit scripsisse carissimum fratrem suum Paulum. Magnus item Dionysius quaedam ex hac epistola ad Hebraeos citat tanquam a Paulo praeceptore suo deprompta. Idem similiter comprobant Clemens primus, Innocentius primus, Ambrosius, Chrysostomus, Gregorius Nazianzenus, Damascenus, Isidorus et alii multi catholici doctores. Nec verum est semper dubitatum esse de auctore huius epistolae ad Hebraeos, cum scribat Origenes, quod ante tempora sua omnes antiqui et maiores eam ut Pauli apostoli suscipiebant. Mira autem arrogantia atque pertinacia est huius scriptoris, quod, ubi tot catholici doctores pontifices concilia declarant hanc epistolam esse Pauli et idem universalis ecclesiae usus ac consensus comprobat, hic scriptor adhuc dubitat, tanquam toto orbe prudentior. *De secunda Petri diu*

not necessarily to denote the author, but to denote the aim of the book, in the same manner that the writings prelude the Psalms [53].

The passage in John 7.53—8.11, of the woman taken in adultery, is a good illustration of Erasmus' early boldness in historical criticism, followed by his later caution under the pressure of the Church. He wrote that this history of the woman taken in adultery is not

---

dubitatum est. Hanc epistolam sub nomine beati, Petri etiam iam olim ecclesia suo usu recepit et definitione conciliorum Laudicensis, Carthaginensis tertii, Gelasii papae nec non et decreto Innocentii magni. Praeterea ex eiusdem epistolae littera patet eam a beato Petro esse scriptam. Nam illius scriptor Petrus apostolus in principio nominatur et adfuisse dominicae transfigurationi asseritur in eadem epistola; soli autem tres ex apostolis (ut evangelistae testantur) illi adstiterunt; unde cum nec Iacobum maiorem nec Ioannem evangelistam eam scripsisse in confesso sit, recte conficitur Petrum illam scripsisse. His itaque perspectis inepte et sine ullo fructu de eius auctore dubitatum esse proponitur, cum modo nulli liceat haesitare quin illa beati sit Petri. *De apocalypsi diu dubitatum est, non dico ab haereticis, sed ab orthodoxis viris; qui scriptum tamen ut a spiritu sancto profectum amplectebantur, de scriptoris nomine incerti.* Liber apocalypsis aperte cognoscitur a beato Ioanne apostolo et evangelista editus tum ex ecclesiae usu, tum ex eiusdem definitione in conciliis, Carthaginensis tertio atque beati Gelasii pariterque in synodo Toletana; in qua dicitur: Apocalypsis librum multorum conciliorum auctoritas et synodica sanctorum praesulum Romanorum decreta Ioannis evangelistae esse praescribunt et inter divinos libros recipiendum constituerunt. Cui quidem synodo insigni doctrina praefulgens interfuit Isidorus praesul Hispalensis. Praeterea ex eiusdem libri contextu ostenditur beatus Ioannes illius auctor; nam in illa scriptor esse dicitur Ioannes, qui perhibuit testimonium verbo dei quique ea de causa in Pathmon insulam relegatus est; quae profecto de alio a Ioanne apostolo et evangelista nequeunt intelligi. Idem rursus contestantur sacerrimus pater Dionysius Areopagita beati Pauli discipulus, Innocentius primus, Irenaeus, Iustinus, Damascenus aliique catholici doctores et sancti viri; inter quos splendidum ecclesiae iubar Augustinus hoc manifeste indicat; qui alogios sive alogos inter haereticos ab ecclesia damnatos connumerat, eo quod Ioannem apostolum et evangelistam negent evangelium scripsisse et apocalypsim. Quapropter eodem modo lapsus est hic scriptor in ista propositione, ut in praecedentibus propositionibus, praemissum dubium proponendo pusillis praebens offendiculum, omissa explicatione determinationis ecclesiae, sacrorum conciliorum et sanctorum patrum."

53) Ibid., "Praecipuus auctor scripturae canonicae est spiritus sanctus. Quam diu de illo non dubitatur, non potest omnino vacillare scripturarum auctoritas neque frigere piorum hominum lectio, per quodcunque organum illam nobis porrexerit. Quanquam non protinus, quicquid receptum est usu ecclesiastico, obligat nos ad credendum, tanquam articulum fidei. Titulos recepit ecclesia, nimirum utens vulgo receptis ad indicandum, quod opus designet. Quemadmodum citantur apocrypha, cum aliorum innumerabilium,

79

found in the majority of the Greek manuscripts [54], yet he reinserted this passage in the later editions of his New Testament.

The result of Erasmus' critical study of the Canon can be seen in the *Ratio ... ad veram theologiam,* where Erasmus has a graduation of authority in the scriptural books. He says that Isaiah is more important than Judith or Hester, that Matthew is more significant than the Revelation ascribed to John, that the Epistles of Paul to the Romans and Corinthians hold more weight than the Epistle written to the Hebrews [55].

---

tum Hieremiae, non quod sint Hieremiae, sed quod illius nomine prodita sint. Ita dicitur liber Iob, non quod ille scripserit, sed quod de illo tractet. Similiter dicitur liber Thobiae. Titulus itaque non semper notat auctorem. Quemadmodum non omnes psalmi putantur esse David, qui titulum habent nominis illius. *Quod si universalis ecclesia hac mente recipit titulos ut pro impiis habeat, qui de homine auctore dubitant, manibus ac pedibus discedo in illius sententiam meumque intellectum captivo in obsequium fidei.* Nam iuxta sensum humanum nec credo epistolam ad Hebraeos esse Pauli aut Lucae nec secundam Petri esse Petri nec apocalypsim esse Ioannis apostoli, qui scripsit evangelium. Possem hic multa argumenta congerere; sed praestat vitare infirmorum offendiculum. *Nam plus apud me valet expressum ecclesiae iudicium, quam ullae rationes humanae.* Solus ille scrupulus habet animum meum, an ecclesia receperit titulos, ut non solum velit haberi pro indubitatis, quae in his libris scripta sunt, verum pariter exigat, ut pro indubitato habeamus ab his auctoribus esse profecta, quorum titulos gerunt. Id si est damno ac reiicio dubitationem meam omnem, quae ne fuit quidem ulla, si ea mens est ecclesiae ex afflatu spiritus sancti. Quanquam theologi fatentur totam ecclesiam errare posse in his duntaxat, quae non requiruntur necessario ad salutem gregis; quo de genere fortassis est titulus. Alioqui si tantopere urgemur titulis vel usu receptis vel in concilio quopiam recitatis, cogemur librum ad Paulam et Eustochium de assumptione sacratissimae virginis credere esse conscriptum ab Hieronymo. Et in concilio Carthaginensi, cui interfuit Augustinus, velut et in epistola Innocentii, quinque libri tribuuntur Solomoni, proverbia, canticum canticorum, ecclesiastes, ecclesaiasticus et sapientia; cum ecclesiasticus apud Hebraeos non sit in canone et sapientia nusquam exstiterit apud Hebraeos, sed Philonis est credatur, qui Graeca polluit eloquentia."

54) LB vi, 373. John 7.53. "Historia de muliere adultera non habetur in plerisque Graecis exemplaribus."

55) Holborn, 211.10. "Nec fortassis absurdum fuerit in sacris quoque voluminibus ordinem auctoritatis aliquem constituere, id quod facere non est veritus Augustinus. Nam primae debentur iis libris, de quibus numquam fuit addubitatum a veteribus. Apud me certe plus habet ponderis Isaias quam Iudith aut Esther, plus euangelium Matthaei quam Apocalypsis inscripta Ioanni, plus epistolae Pauli ad Romanos et Corinthios quam epistola scripta ad Hebraeos."

Cf. *Ecclesiastes,* LB v, 1049. See footnote 27.

The effect of Erasmus' Canon evaluation on his work can be noted by his omitting to paraphrase the book of Revelation, the only book in the New Testament that he failed to paraphrase. In writing to Gerard de la Roche he says,

"I have completed the paraphrases of all the books in the New Testament with the exception of the book of Revelation, which by no means detracts from the *Paraphrases*, since it is a book interpreted only with difficulty and moreover I believe does not possess the dignity of this work" [56].

In his historical critical approach, both to the text itself and in his work with the Canon, Erasmus is a champion for the cause of historical criticism. As Wilhelm Maurer has so well stated:

"Man kann zusammenfassend sagen: im wesentlichen hat Erasmus alles Rüstzeug innerer und äusserer Kritik, über das ein moderner Historiker verfügt, schon bei der Hand" [57].

In Luther's position on the Canon we find that he is not so interested in the historical approach as he is in the theological meaning of the work [58]. While Erasmus' main emphasis rested on the style of the text, or the *innerer Kritik*, Luther's primary interest lies in the message of the text. Erasmus was much influenced by humanism on this point and therefore his primary interest was in investigation and critical appraisal, while Luther's interest was in the theological significance of the text.

To illustrate this principle of Luther's we have only to look at the preface to his translation of the New Testament. Here he lists the New Testament writings that he thinks are the most important. First, he says, come the Gospel of John, and the Epistles of Saint Paul, particularly that to the Romans, and the first Epistle of Saint Peter. These are "der rechte Kern und Mark unter allen Büchern". All Christians are advised to read and know these books through daily reading as their daily bread. The Gospel of John is "das

---

56) Allen, 1432.27. "Etenim praeter alia multa, absolui Paraphrases omnes in Nouum Testamentum; excepta Apocalypsi, quae nullo modo recipit paraphrasten, vix etiam interpretem, vt iam illam hoc labore dignam ducerem."

57) "Luthers Verständnis des Neutestamentlichen Kanons", Fuldaer Hefte, Berlin, 1960. p. 56.

58) Maurer, op. cit., p. 62. "Es ist klar: in allen diesen Fällen geht Luther nicht von einem historischen, sondern von einem dogmatischen Bild des Apostolates aus."

einzige, zarte, rechte Hauptevangelium". Its contents are the words
of Christ, which give life, where as the other Gospels tell more of
his miracles and are not as helpful for living today. Also important
are Saint Paul's and Saint Peter's Epistles, and to a lesser degree,
the three Gospels: Matthew, Mark and Luke. In summation, the
most important New Testament books are the Gospel of John, and
his first Epistle, the Epistles of Saint Paul, namely Romans, Galatians, and Ephesians, and Saint Peter's first Epistle[59].

In his discussion of the *antilegomena* Luther knew Erasmus'
Canon criticism, for he had available Erasmus' edition of the New
Testament, yet he doesn't seem unduly influenced by it. He made
use of it as we shall see, but his presuppositions were different from
those of Erasmus, mainly because the historical aspects of doubtful
authorship of some of the writings had little effect on him, and
this historical study was not in the least a criterion for him as it
was for Erasmus.

---

59) WA (Deutsch Bibel), 6.1.12. "Darumb ist auffs erste zu wissen, das
abtzuthun ist der wahn, das vier Euangelia und nur vier Euangelisten sind,
und gantz zuverwerffen, das etlich des newen testaments bucher teyllen, ynn
legales, historiales, Prophetales, und sapientiales, vermeynen damit (weyss
nicht wie) das newe, dem alten testament zuuergleychen, Sondern festiglich
zu halten, das gleych wie das allte testament ist eyn buch, darynnen Gottis
gesetz und gepot, da neben die geschichte beyde dere die selben gehallten
und nicht gehallten haben, geschrieben sind, Also ist das newe testament,
eyn buch, darynnen das Euangelion und Gottis verheyssung, danebe auch
geschichte beyde, dere die dran glewben vnd nit glewben, geschrieben sind,
Also das man gewiss sey, das nur eyn Euangelion sey, gleych wie nur eyn
buch des newen testaments, und nur eyn Gott, der do verheysset. (6.21).
So sehen wyr nu, das nicht mehr, denn ein Euangelion ist, gleych wie nur eyn
Christus, Syntemal Euangelion nichts anders ist noch seyn kan, denn eyn
predigt von Christo Gottis und Dauids son ... Der beschreybts lange, der
viel werck und wort Christi beschreybt, als die vier Euangelisten thun, Der
beschreybts aber kurtz, der nicht von Christus wercken, sondern kurtzlich
antzeygt, wie er durchs sterben und aufferstehen, sund tod und helle uber-
wunden habe, denen die an yhn glawben, wie Petrus vnd Paulus. Darumb
sihe nu drauff, das du nit aus Christo eyn Mosen machist, noch aus dem
Euangelio eyn gesetz oder lere buch, wie bis her geschehen ist, und ettlich
vorrhede auch Sanct Hieronymi sich horen lassen, Denn das Euangeli foddert
eygentlich nicht unser werck, das wyr da mit frum und selig werden, ia es
verdampt solche werck, sondern es foddert nur glawben an Christo. (10.7).
Wilchs die rechten und Edlisten bucher des newen testaments sind. Aus
disem allen kanstu nu recht vrteylen unter allen buchern, und unterscheyd
nehmen, wilchs die besten sind, Denn nemlich ist Johannis Euangelion und
Sanct Paulus Epistelln, sonderlich die zu den Romern, und Sanct Peters erste

Of the seven *antilegomena*, Luther retains only four: the Epistles of James and Jude, the Epistle to the Hebrews, and Revelation [60]. As we review Luther's statements on these it will be easy to notice the immense gulf between the criterion of Luther and Erasmus as to why a book should be canonical or not.

In his preface to the Epistle to the Hebrews in the *Deutsch Bibel* Luther stated,

> "First, it has been pointed out that this Epistle to the Hebrews was not written by Paul or any other Apostle ... It seems to me it is a case of an Epistle being put together from many fragments, and is not of the same standard throughout ... Who wrote this Epistle is unknown, and probably will remain so. But this is not the matter in question. *The teaching of the Epistle is what should concern us*" [61].

The Epistle of Jude, as that of Hebrews, did not come under any violent attack from Luther. He stated in his preface to it *(Deutsch Bibel)* that it was undoubtedly an extract from the second Epistle

---

Epistel der rechte kern und marck unter allen buchern, wilche auch billich die ersten seyn sollten, Und eym iglichen Christen zu ratten were, das er die selben am ersten und aller meysten lese, und yhm durch teglich lessen so gemeyn mechte, als das teglich brott, Denn ynn disen findistu nicht viel werck und wunderthatten Christi beschrieben, Du findist aber gar meysterlich ausgestrichen, wie der glawbe an Christum, sund, tod und helle uberwindet, und das leben, gerechtigkeyt und seligkeit gibt, wilchs die rechte artt ist des Euangeli, wie du gehoret hast. — Denn wo ich lieber der werck, denn seyner predigt mangelln, Denn die werck hulffen myr nichts, aber seyne wort die geben das leben, wie er selbs sagt. Weyl nu Johannes gar wenig werck von Christo, aber gar viel seyner predigt schreybt, widderumb die andern drey Euangelisten viel seyner werck, wenig seyner wort beschreyben, ist Johannis Euangelion das eynige zartte recht hewbt Euangelion und den andern dreyen weyt fur zu zihen und hoher zu heben, Also auch Sanct Paulus und Petrus Epistelln, weyt uber die drey Euangelia Matthei, Marci und Luce furgehen. — Summa, Sanct Johannis Euangeli und seyne erste Epistel, Sanct Paulus Epistel, sonderlich die zu den Romern, Galatern, Ephesern, und Sanct Peters erste Epistel, das sind die bucher, die dyr Christum zeygen, und alles leren, das dyr zu wissen nott und selig ist, ob du schon kein ander buch noch lere nummer sehest noch horist, Darumb ist sanct Jacobs Epistel eyn rechte stroern Epistel gegen sie, denn sie doch keyn Euangelisch art an yhr hat, Doch dauon weytter ynn andern vorrheden."

60) Luther lists these four under the title of doubtful books in his *Deutsch Bibel*. See WA (Deutsch Bibel), 6.1 ff.

61) WA (Deutsch Bibel), 7.344.4. "Und auffs erst, das dise Epistel zu den Ebreern nicht Sanct Paulus noch eynigs Apostel sey, ... Mich dunckt, es sey ein Epistel von vielen stucken zusamen gesetzt, und nicht eynerley ordentlich handele ... Wer sie aber geshrieben hab, ist unbewust, will auch

of Peter, and that both the content and the language show that the author is not the apostle Jude, but it was written at a later date [62].

Luther felt at first that the Epistle of Jude was useless, but later he recognized it to be taken from the writings of Peter, who wrote it in opposition to the Papacy [63].

The Epistle of James was extensively criticised by Luther, a criticism founded entirely upon theological grounds. In his translation of the *Deutsch Bibel* Luther says in his preface to the Epistle of James that all the ancients held this epistle to be doubtful and he upholds their opinion. The Epistle, Luther felt, is filled with the law of God, which he does not hold to be apostolic writing. First, its teaching is in contrast to Saint Paul and all the other New Testament writings, since it ascribes justification to works, saying that Abraham became justified from his works ... Then, the office of a true apostle is to preach of Jesus' suffering and resurrection, and to lay the foundation for faith, as Christ himself says in John 18. And therein all sacred books agree, they all preach Christ. *"And this is the proper proofstone for judging all books, if they teach Christ, or not ..."*. Luther disposed of James by calling it *eine rechte stroherne Epistel* [64].

---

wol unbewust bleyben noch eyn weyle, da ligt aucht nichts an, Uns soll benugen an der lere, die er so bestendiglich aus und ynn der schrifft grundet, Und gleych, eyn rechten feynen gryff und mas zeygt, die schrifft zu lesen und handelln."

62) Ibid., 7.386.22. "Die Epistel aber Sanct Judas, kan niemant leugnen, das eyn austzog oder abschrifft ist aus Sanct Peters ander Epistel, so der selben alle wort fast gleych sind ... Datzu so ist der Apostel Iudas ynn kriechische sprach nit domen, sondern ynn Persenlandt, als man sagt, das er ia nicht kriechissch hatt geschrieben."

63) WA, 7.755.4. "Breviter Epistola Iudae, mihi quondam inutilis visa, nunc agnita est e Petri Epistola sumpta, propter solum Papam esse scripta. Uterque enim indicat, quod subintrabunt, id est, iuxta Euangelium sua inferent et, ut ait Petrus, subintroducent, id est, iuxta introducent sectas, manifeste eorum insidiosas et fallaces illusiones, quibus retento nomine Euangelii et Christi sua potius tradunt indicantes."

64) WA (Deutsch Bibel), 6.10.33; 7, 384.1. "Die Epistel Sanct Jacobi, wie woll sie von den allten verworffen ist, lobe ich und halt sie doch fur gutt, darumb, das sie gar keyn menschen lere setzt und Gottis gesetz hart treybt, Aber, das ich meyn meynung drauff stelle, doch on ydermans nachteyl, acht ich sie fur keyns Apostel schrifft, und ist das meyn ursach. — Auffs erst, das sie stracks widder Sanct Paulos und alle ander schrifft, den wercken die rechtfertigung gibt, und spricht, Abraham sey aus seynen wercken rechtfertigt

In another statement on the Epistle of James, Luther shows that in all probability he was acquainted with Erasmus' statements on the authenticity of James. In much the same words as Erasmus, Luther fails to find apostolic majesty or a mode comparable to Paul's, for Paul speaks of living by faith and for James, faith without works is dead [65].

In disputing the number of sacraments in the *Babylonian Captivity of the Church*, Luther again argues against the canonicity of the Epistle of James. The Roman church had built their case for the rite of extreme unction on the passage in James 5.14 ff. Luther argues that it is impossible to found a sacrament on this passage, for this epistle was not written by the Apostle James nor does it have apostolic dignity, as many had already asserted [66]. In his preaching on the Epistle of first Peter, Luther gives his prerequisites for a canonical book, adding that the Epistle of James does not meet these standards [67].

---

worden, ... Denn das ampt eyns rechten Apostel ist, das er von Christus leyden und aufferstehen und ampt predige, und lege des selben glawbens grund, wie er selb sagt Johan. 18. yhr werdet von myr zeugen, Und daryn stymmen alle rechtschaffene heylige bucher uber eyns, das sie alle sampt Christum predigen und treyben, Auch ist das der rechte prufesteyn alle bucher zu taddelln, wenn man sihet, ob sie Christum treyben, odder nit."

65) WA 2.425.10. "Quod autem Iacobi Apostoli epistola inducitur 'Fides sine operibus mortua est' (James 2.17), primum stilus epistolae illius longe est infra Apostolicam maiestatem nec cum Paulino ullo modo comparandus, deinde de fide viva loquitur Paulus."
Cf. Erasmus, LB vi, 1038. "Nec enim referre videtur usquequaque majestatem illam et gravitatem Apostolorum."

66) Ibid., 6.568.1. *De captivitate Babylonica ecclesiae.* "Omitto enim, quod hanc Epistolam non esse Apostoli Iacobi, nec apostolico spiritu dignam, multi valde probabiliter asserant, licet consuetudine auctoritatem, cujuscunque sit, obtinuerit. Tamen, si etiam esset Apostoli Iacobi, dicerem, non licere Apostolum sua auctoritate sacramentum instituere ..."

67) Ibid., 12.268.17 ff. Epistel Sanct Petri gepredigt und ausgelegt. "Darauss kan man aber urteylen, was eyn rechtschaffen Christlich leere odder predig sey. Denn wenn man wil das Evangelium predigen, so muss es kurtz umb sein von der aufferstehung Christi. Wer das nicht predigt, der is keyn Apostel. Denn das ist das hewbtstuck unssers glawbens. Und das sind die rechschaffen edlisten bücher, die solchs am meysten leren und treyben, wie oben gesagt ist. Darumb kan man wol spüren, das die Epistel Jacobi keyn rechte Apostolisch Epistel ist."
The date of this lecture is 1522. Note that this is almost identical with the *Deutsch Bibel* date. The problem of the authenticity of the Canon was predominant at this time.

The fourth book that Luther places in the "doubtful" category is the book of Revelation.

> "As to the revelation of John, I let everyone think as he pleases, and I do not wish to bind anyone to an opinion or argument. I say what I feel, for to me this work excludes various things, so that I hold it neither apostolic nor prophetic. First and foremost, the Apostles do not deal with visions, but rather with clear, blunt words of prophecy, like Peter and Paul, and like Christ in the Gospels also does, as is becoming to the apostolic office, telling clearly without images or visions about Christ and his work ... *Therefore I must keep to the books that bring Christ to me bright and plainly*" [68].

In conclusion, the authenticity of the Canon for Luther rests primarily in the theological doctrine of the books and in whether or not they teach Christ. Though Luther, like Erasmus, will use historical arguments, these arguments are only of secondary importance. The fact is that Luther had his own ideas as to what was canonical and what was not, and his criterion for canonical authenticity was always grounded on theological presuppositions. Against Erasmus he would write in the *De servum arbitrium* that "Scripture simply acknowledges the trinity of God, the humanity of Christ, and the unforgiven sinner; nothing is obscure or ambiguous" [69].

Thirdly, Erasmus' use of the Church Fathers plays an important part in his concept of erudition. He gives to the Fathers a very important place in his theory of interpretation [70]. Erasmus was convinced that the Church Fathers were the answer to the problems

---

68) WA (Deutsch Bibel), 7.704. "Vorrhede auff die offinbarung Sanct Johannis. An diesem buch der offinbarung Johannis, las ich auch yderman seynes synnes walden, will niemant an meyn dunckel odder vrteyl verpunden haben, Ich sage was ich fule, Myr mangellt an disem buch nit eynerley, das ichs wider Apostolisch noch prophetisch hallte, Auffs erst und aller meyst, das die Apostell nicht mit gesichten umbgehen, sondern mit klaren und durren wortten weyssagen, wie Petrus, Paulus, Christus ym Euangelio auch thun, denn es auch dem Apostolischen ampt gepurt, klerich und on bild odder gesicht von Christo und seynem thun zu reden ... Darumb bleyb ich bey den buchern, die myr Christum hell und reyn der geben."

69) WA, 16.608. "Scriptura simpliciter confitetur trinitatem Dei et humanitatem Christi et peccatum irremissibile, nihil hic obscuritalis aut ambiguitatis."

70) Ernst Stacheline, *Erasmus u. Ökolampad in ihrem Ringen um die Kirche Jesu Christi* (Gedenkschrift zum 400. Todestage Erasmus von Rotterdam), Basel, 1936, p. 167. "Auch durch die Erschliessung dieses Kirchenvaters sollte der 'instauratio pietates' gedient werden: 'aurem flumen habet, lo-

that arose from interpretation. Through the erudition of the Fathers, Erasmus saw the means to understand the difficulties that arose in exegesis. The Fathers brightened and clarified the Scripture so that it is possible to understand the text. Here again we see the importance of erudition for Erasmus. What was beyond the learning of Erasmus was not beyond the learning of the Fathers, or better stated, the erudition of the Fathers could be utilized to supplement the erudition that one possessed.

It is a cycle that Erasmus repeats and repeats: study in order to become more learned, and the more learning we possess the more qualified we are to grasp the highest form of learning, or to put it another way, erudition leads to more erudition, which is finally a knowledge of the Holy Scriptures. *Bonae Litterae*, if properly used, leads to a knowledge of *Sacras Litteras*.

The Fathers are the illuminators and clarifiers of the text, moreover they are the co-workers in erudition that help to penetrate the deeper meanings of the Biblical text[71]. The Fathers also clarify arguments that arise from interpretation of the Scriptures, and help to correct errors that arise in interpretation[72]. Moreover, when a

---

cupletissimam bibliothecam habet, quisquis unum habet Hieronymum', (Erasmus to Wm. Warham in dedication to his edition of Jerome. Allen II, p. 219 ff.) ... nach den Evangelien und den apostolischen Schriften sei niemand würdiger als er, von den Christen gelesen zu werden."
Cf. Allen, 186.8 "Obsecro te, mi Francisce, per mutuam charitatem nostram et per faelicitatem tuam, quae mihi non minus curae est quam mea, vt toto pectore incumbas in sacras literas; euolue veteres interpretes. Crede mihi, aut hac via perueniemus ad beatitudinem, aut nunquam perueniemus."

71) *Ratio ... ad veram Theologiam*, Holborn, 295.15. "Immo partem laboris adimat nobis veterum labor, adiuvemur illorum commentariis, dummodo primum ex his deligamus optimos, velut Origenem, qui sic est primus, ut nemo cum illo conferri possit, post hunc Basilium, Nazianzenum, Athanasium, Cyrillum, Chrysostomum, Hieronymum, Ambrosium, Hilarium, Augustinum; ..."
Cf. ibid., 292.1. "Quandoquidem haec non Origeni tantum, sed et Augustino optima ratio est interpretandi divinas litteras, si locum obscurum ex aliorum locorum collatione reddamus illustrem et mysticam scripturam mystica, sacra sacram exponat.
Cf. *Methodus*, ibid., 160.18. "Adiuvemur illorum commentariis, dum modo primum ex his deligamus optimos, velut Origenem, qui sic est primus, ut nemo cum illo conferri possit, Basilium, Nazianzenum, Athanasium, Cyrillum, Chrysostomum, Hieronymum, Ambrosium, Hilarium, Augustinum, deinde ut hos ipsos cum delectu iudicioque legat."

72) Allen, 1342.941. "Hic rursum appello meum aequum iudicem, quum hoc scripserim ante proditum Lutheri dogma, quum idem sentiant omnes

theological problem arose, Erasmus turned to the exposition of the Fathers to expedite a solution.

Erasmus gave importance to the Fathers because of three underlying factors: first and primarily, because they were so important to his concept of erudition; secondly, because the Fathers represented that combination of good learning and good theology that Erasmus was seeking to establish in place of the Scholastic theology of his day; and thirdly, because the Fathers were approved by the Church[73]. This third factor became more important to Erasmus as he became involved in more and more theological discussions.

It is not necessary to dwell at length here on points one and two, point one having been discussed in the preceding sections, and point two being contained in the whole cause of *bonae litterae* or the Renaissance fight against Scholasticism.

But in discussing point three it is well to keep in mind points one and two: the use of the Fathers in erudition and their use to displace Scholasticism. Of course there is a connection between these two points because to bring the Fathers into a place of prime importance leaves little room for the Scholastic teachings; for the Fathers, some in particular, were well versed in both sacred and secular literature; this in itself opening new areas of study that would be outside Scholasticism as such.

However point three is very important for our discussion, for as we shall see, Erasmus' use of the Church Fathers because they are approved by the Church leads us to his catholic position[74].

---

theologi tum veteres tum recentes, Origines, Hieronymus, Chrysostomus, Hilarius, Arnobius, Scotus, Thomas, cur ego, velut autor huius sententiae, vocor in ius?"

Cf. Allen, 778.18. "Nisi me defenderem, Augustinum, Ambrosium, Athenasium, Chrysostomum, breuiter ceteros othodoxos omneis atque ipsum adeo Hieronymum in communi crimine fuerim deserturus."

73) Ibid., 1342.926. "In Paraphrasi qua explico nonum caput Apostoli Pauli ad Romanos, tribuo minimum quiddam libero arbitrio, videlicet sequutus Originem et Hieronymum. Principio quum paraphrasis sit commentarii genus, quum profitear me in plerisque sequi probatos ac priscos interpretes, quid admissum est piaculi, si sequor alicubi Originem et Hieronymum, autors, vt arbitror, in sacris literis non aspernandos?"

74) For our discussion the term "catholic position" in the relation between the authority of the Scriptures and the authority of the Fathers can be summarized as an "and" relationship (Scriptures *and* Tradition). H. Østergaard-Nielsen (*Scriptura Sacra et Viva Vox*, p. 27) has termed this a "metaphysische Theologie" and defined this as "nicht die Schrift als einzige Autorität festhalten können. Man war gezwungen zu sagen: Bibel und Kirche oder

Erasmus always used the Fathers and loved their commentaries, but how much dependence does he put on them because they were approved by the Church? Let us say that Erasmus' conception of the Fathers was always toward a catholic position, but that Erasmus grows more orthodox when under attack.

Erasmus' catholic position did not stem from the fact that he was trying to agree with the established church but rather from the fact that these ancient theologians answered his demands of *bonae litterae* and at the same time represented an effective instrument in his fight with the Scholastic system. It would be interesting to see what Erasmus' exact position would have been had not Luther appeared on the scene, for, though Erasmus loved the Fathers, especially Jerome, he was not particularly inclined toward Augustine [75] until he was forced to use Augustine in the Free Will controversy. By the time of his *Hyperaspistes II*, he says that he is in full agreement with Augustine on grace in relation to the freedom of the will [76].

We can see this change over the position of authority of the Fathers taking place in Erasmus' writings. In *De libero arbitrio diatribe* he stresses the agreement of the Fathers along with the thirteen hundred years' tradition of the Church over against those who stress individuality in interpretation and claim for themselves special illumination and inspiration in interpreting the Scriptures [77].

Bibel und Glaubensbekenntnis oder Bibel und Bekenntnisschriften, ..."
However, Wilhelm Maurer (op. cit., p. 53) has a more definitive definition when he states, "Im Humanismus wird das 'Nebeneinander' Schrift und Tradition zuerst erkannt und zum Massstab des Kanonverständnisses gemacht. Die vorherige Entwicklung der Kirche ist gekennzeichnet durch ein 'Ineinander'."

75) Opuscula, *Hieronymi Stridonensis Vita*, 1233. "Gregorio tribuunt tropologiam, Ambrosio allegoriam, Augustino anagogen; Hieronymo, ne nihil habeat, relinquunt litteram et sensus grammaticum."

76) *Hyperispistes II*, LB x, 1358 e. "Ego cum Augustino gratiam jungo cum libero arbitrio."

77) *De libero arbitrio*, LB ix, 1248 c. "... jam velim illud expendat Lector, num aequum censeat, damnata sententia tot Ecclesiae Doctorum, quam tot jam seculorum ac gentium consensus approbavit, recipere paradoxa quaedam, ob quae nunc tumultuatur orbis Christianus."

Østergaard-Nielsen (op. cit., p. 28) says: "Mag man nun Erasmus als Repräsentant der Katholischen Kirche anerkennen oder nicht, so ist der Autoritätsbegriff doch für Erasmus und die Katholische Kirche der gleiche und beide stehen daher — gemeinsam mit aller protestantischen metaphysischen

But in his defense against Luther's *De servum arbitrium*, Erasmus is even more orthodox when he states that what has been transmitted by the general consent of the orthodox doctors and what has been clearly defined by the Church must no longer be debated and disputed, but believed [78].

It is difficult to determine Erasmus' exact position on this point, for he says that the first authority is the jurisdiction of the ancient Synods . . . followed by the interpreters of authority that the Church has approved [79]. Then on the following page, Erasmus says that the Church receives the writings of the Fathers not as Canonical Scripture, for this is authority irrefutable *(auctoritatis irrefutabilis)*, but as the commentaries of erudite and good men [80].

It would seem from these two statements that Erasmus, when speaking of the Scripture itself, always places it as the irrefutable authority, and the Fathers can never be the final authority. But when speaking in the context of the Church he assumes a very catholic position and uses the *auctoritas* of the Middle Ages [81] in order to present himself in an orthodox position. Because Erasmus was caught between all sides in the violent struggles of his day it is rather hard to pin him down, for one can be sure he will state an orthodox position. In the event he is challenged on his position he always manages to slip his own beliefs into his writings. Here Erasmus, no doubt under the influence of the Reformation, has placed the Scripture as the final and irrefutable authority, yet preceding this statement, he is careful to say that he has an orthodox view.

There is one final point on the Fathers that should be elaborated on in greater detail in order to better understand the hermeneutic

---

Theologie — vereint gegen Luther in der Frage, die für ihn die entscheidende war, nämlich, die Frage nach der Klarheit oder der Dunkelheit der Schrift."

78) *Hyperaspistes I,* LB x, 1259 d. ". . . quod ab Orthodoxis omnibus magno consensu traditum est, quod Ecclesia clara voce definit, non jam disputandum, sed credendum."

79) *Catechesis,* LB v, 1171 f. "Prima est veterum Synodorum auctoritas . . . Huic succedit interpretum auctoritis, quorum et sanctimoniam consecravit Ecclesia, et libros approbavit."

80) *Ibid.,* 1172 e. ". . . non ut Canonicam scripturam, hoc est auctoritatis irrefutabilis, sed ut eruditorum ac bonorum virorum Commentarios."

81) The *auctoritas* of the Middle Ages included not only the Scripture but also that which spoke for the Scriptures (lingua ipsa Scriptura) such as the *Glossa ordinaria.* cf. Peter Lombard, IV Sent., d. 4.

of Erasmus: the relationship of Jerome to Augustine. Here Erasmus lays open his mind and deepest thoughts, which gives more insights into the development of his hermeneutic than many of his writings.

Jerome is one of Erasmus' greatest heroes, if not the greatest. Both Jerome's elegant style [82] and his undogmatic form of Christianity appealed to the personality of Erasmus. In fact Erasmus saw Jerome as the ancient champion of all that he considered *bonae litterae*. Moreover it was Jerome's great interest in and knowledge of the Scriptures that had a special appeal to a man that was to follow in Jerome's footsteps. In his dedication to *Hieronymi Opera*, Erasmus wrote to William Warham, "How unsatisfied I am with myself when I perceive the piety and erudition of this man in his writings, when I view his enthusiasm in study, when I see his wonderful knowledge and retention of the contents of the Sacred Scriptures" [83]. Included herein are Erasmian principles of *ad fontes, bonae litterae,* and *erudition.*

Jerome was not interested in systematic theology as such, and this to Erasmus was the crowning point, for Erasmus saw Jerome

---

82) Allen, 325.65. "Siquidem vnum habemus Hieronymum quem in diuinis litteris Graeciae pessimus opponere."
Cf. *Methodus*, Holborn, 161.6. "At Hieronymus ita deliciis omnia condit ac locupletat, ut cum aberrat a vero, cum a re digreditur, tamen plus bonae rei doceat quam isti, cum vere rem tradunt, ut ne dicam interim, quod omnino tales ipsi reddimur, cuiusmodi sunt auctores, in quibus assidue versamur. Neque enim perinde ciborum qualitas transit in corporis habitum ut lectio in animum ac mores. Si in ieiunis, in frigidis, in fucatis, in spinosis ac rixosis scriptoribus assidui simus, tales evadamus oportet. Sin in iis, qui vere spirant Christum, qui ardent, qui vivunt, qui veram pietatem et docent et praestant, hos saltem aliqua ex parte referemus."
Ibid., 162.5. "Denique malim cum Hieronymo pius esse theologus quam cum Scoto invictus."
83) Allen, 396.123. "Sin doctrina exigas, queso te, quem habet vel eruditissima Graecia sie absolutum in omni doctrinae genere vt cum Hieronymo sic committendus? Quis vnquam pari felicitate omneis totius eruditionis parteis coniunxit et absoluit? Quis vunquam in tot linguis antecelluit vnus? Cui tanta historiarum, tanta geographiae, tanta antiquitatis noticia contigit vnquam? Quis vnquam sacrarum et prophanarum omnia litterarum et parum et absolutam scientiam est assecutus? Sin memoriam examines, quis author seu vetus seu nouus quem ille non in promptu habuerit? ... Quis sic vniuersam Diuinam Scripturam edidicit, imbibit, concoxit, versauit, meditatus est? Quis aeque sudavit in omni doctrinae genere? Iam si morum sanctimoniam spectes, quis Christum spiret viuidius? Quis docuit ardentius?

not only as the champion of *bonae litterae* but moreover the champion of the *philosophia Christi*. Preserved Smith, one of the best of the English biographers of Erasmus, has observed this deep admiration of Erasmus for Jerome:

> "In the hermit of Bethlehem who translated the Scriptures, who cultivated the tongues, who loved the classics, who cared so little for systematic theology and so much for life, Erasmus saw the prototype of his own mind and the champion of the 'Philosophy of Christ'" [84].

With such a predilection for Jerome, Augustine naturally would have little appeal for Erasmus. In the *Hieronymi Stridonensis Vita* Erasmus compares these "two princes of the ancient Church", giving the advantage to Jerome without being unkind to Augustine: "Jerome has displayed more eloquence, Augustine more dialectic." This emphasis on the importance of *eloquentia* ties in closely with *eruditio* [85]. The mere fact that Erasmus places more importance on style than on substance in this comparison is symptomatic of the way Erasmus viewed the two men: one a man of *belles lettres*, the

---

Cf. ibid., 141.16 (1500). "Flagrat iam olim mihi incredibili ardore animus Hieronymianas epistolas commentariis illustrandi, et nescio quis Deus mihi pectus accendit agitque vt rem tantam et a nullo hactenus tentatem audeam animo concipere. Mouet me viri coelestis et omnium Christianorum sine controuersia longe tum doctissimi tum facundissimi pietas; cuius scripta cum digna sint quae ab omnibus passim legantur et ediscantur, vix pauci legant, pauciores mirantur, paucissimi intelligunt."

84) Preserved Smith, op. cit., p. 191.

85) *Opuscula*, "Hieronymi Vita", 1255. "Franciscus Philelphus, arrepta velut censoria virgula, Augustino tribuit dialecticae palmam, eloquentiae Hieronymo; non est meum Augustini laudibus quicquam decerpere: verum illud ipsa res calamitat, Hieronymum, Augustino non minus eruditione superiorem fuisse quam dicendi laude. Siquidem Hieronymus, Graeci sermonis callentissimus, non modo totum Aristotelem, sed ceteros item philosophos omnes euoluerat; Augustinos, id quod et ipse fatetur et indicant libri, duos dumtaxat Aristotelis libellos, tum forte in Latinum versos sermonem, de Praedicamentis, ac de Enunciatione. Et, vt ingenue dicam, argumentatur aliquanto perplexius ac molestius Augustinus: at quanto solidius, quanto aliis neruis Hieronymus? Mihi videtur vterque vtraque facultate mirabilis, sed eloquentiam magis ostentauit Hieronymus, dialecticen Augustinus. Quamquam ego nec de vitae genere prorsus accedo Philelphi iudicio. In se quidem rigidior Hieronymus quam Augustinus, at in alios lenior; nec vnquam Hieronymus a suis exegit fratribus, quod a suis clericis Augustinus. Sed praestat omittere collationem inter duos Ecclesiae Latinae proceres, pro quorum eximiis virtutibus magis decet agere gratias Deo, quam excitare contentionem inter studiosos."

other a man more noted for the depth of his theological approach. Both are erudite men, but Erasmus chooses the more eloquent in expression [86].

The fact that Erasmus gives such a high place to the Fathers in this matter of interpretation also adds to Erasmus' historical relativism. In the former sections on relativism, Erasmus' emphasis was on making the text pertinent for his day, and this led to his relativizing the text. But in his consideration of the Fathers, the relativizing comes through quite a different application. In this case the relative value is put on an historical moment in time rather than the present situation, as in the previous case. In the previous point Erasmus had the text answer the questions of his day much in the sense of an apology, but with the Fathers, Erasmus is making the text speak from a certain moment in time. This brings the particular historical exposition of the Fathers into the present situation without benefit of discrimination, thereby relativizing the message of the text itself. Here the Scriptures are not exegeted in the freedom of the Spirit, but rather through the exposition and views of the Church Fathers.

But after all is said and done, if we look behind all the statements that Erasmus makes in the light of the struggles with which he was constantly faced, we see that the purpose of the Fathers for Erasmus was one of erudition. As we have mentioned before, Erasmus was never concerned over how orthodox his arguments were until he was caught in the fire of controversy, and then he was quick to assume an orthodox position, showing himself in agreement with the Church. But in his early works and letters his statements show that though he is always oriented toward a catholic position, he is primarily interested in the Fathers because of their value to erudition.

At the same time, the Fathers are never the final authority in the interpretation of Scripture. Though the Fathers are given a place of high esteem and value by Erasmus in interpreting the Scriptures and though they remain the standard for interpretation, they are never the final authority, for the Holy Scriptures are the

---

86) Erasmus also saw that these two men represented different theological positions, and for his part he would rather not stress these differences at the expense of exciting strife between their followers. Erasmus always stresses peace rather than argument, even if it means foregoing conviction.

final and irrefutable authority for Erasmus, the Scriptures in the light of the exposition of the Fathers.

Since erudition is the means by which Erasmus interprets the Scriptures, it follows that interpretation does not depend on inspiration but on a scientific approach. Such an approach leads to the question of the importance of the Holy Spirit for Erasmus in interpretation of the Scriptures.

First, Erasmus by all means considered the Holy Scriptures to be inspired, and in the *Enchiridion Militis Christiani* he quotes 2 Timothy 16 to show the importance he gives to the inspiration of the Scripture. But it is important for our investigation to examine the context in which he uses this verse. The statement is rendered to show the importance of knowledge:

> "But lest you condemn the help of knowledge *(scientia)* consider this . . . There is no temptation so great that ardent study of the Sacred Scriptures will not easily drive it away, for there is no adversity so sad that it does not render it more bearable . . . all Scripture is divinely inspired and perfected by God the author" [87].

In his catechism Erasmus also gives preeminence to the Scriptures when he states that the Holy Spirit is the author of all Scripture that the Church has pertaining to the Divine, and its authority is inviolable [88]. Here the emphasis lies not only with the inspiration of the Scriptures but also with the authority that they have. The Scriptures are inspired by the Spirit and therefore their authority is invulnerable.

But our quest is in the field of interpretation and Erasmus sees a difference in the fact that the Scriptures are inspired by the Holy Spirit and the use of the Holy Spirit in interpretation. For, although

---

87) Holborn, 30.20. "Sed ne scientiae subsidia contemnas, illud considera . . . Crede mihi, frater animo meo carissime, nulla tam vehemens hostium impressio, id est nulla tam valida tentatio, quam ardens sacrarum litterarum studium non facile retundat, nulla tam tristis adversitas, quam non reddat tolerabilem."

88) LB v, 1167a. "Spiritus autem auctor est omnium Scripturarum, quas pro divinis habet Ecclesia, et quarum inviolabilis est auctoritas."
Cf. LB ix, 863, *Des. Erasmi Declarationes ad censuru facultatis theologiae Parisienis*, in which Erasmus states the medieval principle: "Praecipuus auctor Scripturae canonicae est spiritus sanctus."
Cf. *Apologia*, Holborn, 168.13. "Qui praedicant inviolabilem divinarum scripturarum auctoritatim, . . ."

the Scriptures are inspired, interpretation does not depend on the help of the Spirit [89] but rather on erudition.

The best illustration of erudition as the means to interpretation rather than interpretation's depending on the help of the Holy Spirit is found in Erasmus' tract against Luther, *De libero arbitrio*. Erasmus does not think the question of the freedom of the will, though important, should be allowed to be a question of *articulis fidei* [90], therefore Erasmus' thesis is that in matters where faith is not a question, learning and reason must necessarily play an important part in interpretation. In questions of the nature of the freedom of the will, where Erasmus considered that there was no question as to faith or the authority of the Scriptures, the problem rests on interpretation.

> "I confess that the authority of the Holy Scripture itself is superior to the opinion of all mankind. Truly this concerning the Scriptures is not controversial. Both of us receive and reverence the same Scripture, but the problem concerns the sense of Scripture" [91].

To summarize briefly: interpretation for Erasmus is a matter of erudition that he accomplishes by a philological and historical critical approach to the text, which is supplemented by great reliance on the exposition of the Church Fathers. His conception of the Canon and the authority of the Scripture is greatly influenced by this principle. Erudition, therefore, is the means that Erasmus sees to a correct theory of interpretation.

---

89) Erasmus said that the Bible was written under the direction of the Holy Spirit yet the apostles were not forced into uniformity as to context. *Annotationes*, Matt. 2.7, LB vi, 13. "Ut enim Spiritus ille divinus, mentium apostoliorum moderatur."

90) *Spongia*, LB x, 1651 e. "Quid si Lutherus posthac scribat adversus articulos fidei." This of course says that so far (1523) Luther has not written anything against those points in Christian doctrine that must be believed rather than discussed. When Erasmus challenged Luther it was for Erasmus a theoretical issue rather than a principle of faith.
Cf. ibid., 1663 a. "At pro Luthero proque Lutheri paradoxis nondum est animus mortem oppetere. Non agitur de articulis fidei, sed an principatus Romani Pontificis sit a Christo: an Cardinalium ordo sit necessarium membrum Ecclesiae; an confessio sit ab auctore Christo; ... an ad salutem conducat liberum arbitrium; an sola fides conferat salutem ..."

91) *De libero arbitrio*, LB ix, 1219 b. "Fateor par esse, ut sola divinae Scripturae auctoritas superet omnia mortalium omnia suffragia. Verum hic de Scripturis non est controversia. Utraque pars eamdem Scripturam amplectitur et veneratur: de sensu Scriptura pugna est."

If the term *eruditio* is characteristic of Erasmus' theory of interpretation, then *spiritus* is characteristic of Luther. The results stemming from these two very different ideas of interpretation are very interesting to examine. Erasmus, in *De libero arbitrio*, had stated that there are places in the Sacred Scriptures that God has willed that we should not probe, and if we try to penetrate these we grope in even greater darkness the farther we proceed, so that we recognize the inscrutable majesty of divine wisdom and the weakness of human understanding [92]. Such an approach is a natural outgrowth of a principle of erudition as the governing factor in interpretation.

Luther had answered in his *De servum arbitrium*,

> "What are you asserting, Erasmus? ... either you understand Christ or you don't understand him. How can you believe what you don't understand?" [93]

And again,

> "No one can see the inner clarity of the Scriptures one iota unless the Holy Spirit is given" [94].

In yet another place Luther answers,

> "Therefore you and all Sophists hunt and advance some mysteries that are still hidden in the Scriptures. Truly many secrets are hidden in the Scriptures, not that Scripture is obscure, but in blindness and stupidity of men they cannot see the clear truth" [95].

Luther's point in arguing with Erasmus is that in questions of faith the Holy Scripture is quite clear [96]. It follows that Luther

---

92) Ibid., 1216 c. "Sunt enim in divinis litteris adyta quaedam, in quae Deus noluit nos altius penetrare, et si penetrare conemur, quo fuerimus altius ingressi, hoc magis ac magis caligamus, quo vel sic agnosceremus et divinae sapientiae majestatem impervestigabilem, et humanae mentis imbecillitatem."

93) WA, 18.604. "Quid ais Erasme? ... Christianus vero anathema sit, si non certus sit et assequatur, id quod ei praescribitur: quomodo enim credet; id quod non assequitur?"

94) Ibid., 18.609. "Si de interna claritate dixeris, nullus homo unum iota in scripturis videt, nisi qui spiritum habet."

95) Ibid., 18.607. "Igitur tu et omnes Sophistae, agite et producite unum aliquod mysterium, quod sit in scripturis adhuc abstrusum. Quod vero multis multa manent abstrusa, non hoc sit scripturae obscuritate, sed illorum caecitate vel socordia, qui non agunt, ut clarissimam veritatem videant."

96) Kurt Aland, in his chapter "Martin Luther als Schriftausleger" (Kirchengeschichtliche Entwürfe, Berlin, 1960), says, "Vom unfreien Willen. Denn hier geht es eigentlich darum: gibt die Schrift die Möglichkeit zu einer klaren

could and would state the principle that Scripture is "Ipsa per sese certissima, facillima, apertissima, sui ipsius interpres, omnium omnia probans, iudicans et illuminantes" [97].

Luther won the battle, for the objective critical approach implicit in Erasmus' use of erudition was not what mankind was looking for [98]. Man was searching for faith, and Luther's principle answered that quest.

Antwort auf die Fragen des Glaubens?" (396) ... "In summa: ... Denn keine Frage des Glaubens bleibt in der Schrift im Dunkel, aller Welt ist hier die Botschaft mit Eindringlichkeit und Klarheit gesagt, auch denen, welche nicht Christen sind. Denn an ihrer äusseren Klarheit ist nicht zu rütteln. Zum inneren Verständnis wird jedoch der Geist Gottes erfordert." (400) Calvin also stressed the certainty of the Scriptures, but he formulates the principle differently. The witness of the Holy Spirit gives to the Scriptures the certainty that they deserve. (*Inst.* 1.7.5).

97) WA, 7.97.23. cf. ibid., 7.98.11. "... verba divina esse apertiora et certiora omnia hominum."

98) Luther was very much against the principle of erudition as the means to interpret Scriptures, for he said (Hebräerbriefvorlesung 6.13) that those who attempt to comprehend the Sacred Scriptures and the law of God by their own natural capacity, and to understand them by their own efforts are making a serious mistake.
WA, 54.186.7. "Itaque vehementissime errant, qui sacras literas et legum Dei ingenio suo capere et studio proprio praesumunt intelligere."

Chapter IV

PHILOLOGY AS THE METHOD OF INTERPRETATION

The years immediately preceding and following the year fifteen hundred were a period of discovery. Previously unknown continents were being opened to the nations of Europe, new scientific formulations and inventions were beginning to make themselves felt, and Europe was moving forward from the Middle Ages into a new and less limited world.

But this period was also a period of rediscovery, a discovery as it were of the past glories, age, and principles that Europe was built upon. In its way this rediscovery was also to help Europe burst from the Middle Ages and emerge into what we call the modern period.

All of this did not happen overnight and there was much toil and struggle before Europe finally broke out of the Middle Ages, but the seeds were sown and they were sprouting rapidly, despite the narrow perspective of many of the leaders and peoples of that day. Of course, the Turks were still threatening Europe as the year fifteen hundred began, but the consequences of this period of discovery and rediscovery were so great that never again were a people from the East (if we consider Russia as European) to have the power to threaten Europe.

Erasmus was certainly not a man who could be classified in the same group as the discoverers, for he was neither interested in the new discoveries nor was he able to see their profound consequences. But in the group of men who were interested in the ideal of rediscovery, Erasmus has few equals.

Such a broad critique is helpful here in as much as philology, since it is the method Erasmus used for his rediscovery, is a science of details, and unless we can envision the overall picture, the significance of these details that Erasmus saw as so important will have little consequential value for us. It is, as it were, that if we become too involved in the details we lose sight of the overall picture and fail to realize its significance, just as if we become overly involved in the overall picture we lose sight of the importance of the philological approach that Erasmus did so much to advance.

In viewing Erasmus' philological approach it is also well to keep in mind the fact that Erasmus was developing a rather new science, and that Erasmus himself was basically a man of his times. Certainly his concepts, if viewed from today's more advanced and much more accurate philological methods, fall far short of the highly developed science that we have today.

Neither should Erasmus be viewed from the conclusions that he draws from his philological method, for in such cases as his Latin translation of the New Testament in which he bases his word study wholly on the Greek of the classical period, Erasmus' scholarship falls far short of modern expectations. Erasmus' conclusions and exegesis should not be viewed as goals in themselves, but as they relate to, and help to understand and illustrate, his philological method. All in all it would be better if our minds were not conditioned by twentieth century Biblical scholarship, for it endangers our ability to see the cause that Erasmus championed and the radical nature of such a method for his day.

The philological approach represents a departure from the methodological approach of the Middle Ages, but Erasmus was not the first to develop and utilize this philological approach, for there were others that were instrumental in originating the philological critical method of interpretation. Among these were Laurentius Valla, of whom we shall speak presently, and Faber Stapulensis or Jacques Lefèvre d'Etables, who wrote a commentary on the Pauline letters (*Sancti Pauli Epistulae*, Paris, 1512) [1]. It was this Valla whose *Annotationes Novi Testamenti interpretationem* Erasmus had published in Paris in 1505. And it was against Lefèvre that Erasmus wrote the *Apologia adversus Faber Stapulensis* concerning their disagreement over the correct translation of Hebrews 2.7. Erasmus translated this *Fecisti eum paulisper inferiorem angelis*, while Lefèvre used 'God' instead of 'angels'.

And it is Valla who played such an important part in the development of Erasmus' philological critical method, both from the point of example and teacher of a new art. For Erasmus saw Valla as the champion of the Humanistic cause, a perfect model to follow, and as the genius of a philological approach.

---

1) Cf. Allen, 337.835. "Porro quod admones sciebam, Laurentium Vallam ante nos hoc laboris occupasse, quippe cuius annotationes primus curarim euulgandas; et Iacobi Fabri in Paulinas epistolas commentarios vidi."

Laurentius Valla (1406—1457) exemplified in every way both the very best and the very worst of the Italian Humanism of his century. He was irreligious, a fearless critic of the Roman Church, and possessed a sharp mind that was capable of making his ideas known. It was through his efforts that the *Donatio Constantini* was discredited, and it was his *Annotationes Novi Testamenti interpretationem* that was the first critical study of the text of the New Testament. It is not to be said in his favor that the grounds for such an approach were not inspired by such lofty ideals as was Erasmus, but rather as one of a number of critical appraisals upon all the existing institutions of his day.

It must be said that Erasmus knew very little of the personality and motives of Valla, but only his writings. And these writings had fascinated the young Erasmus [2], particularly since at this time in his life Erasmus was struggling with the Monastic life at Steyn, as well as the typical drabness that was the Middle Ages.

Later, in his travels Erasmus came across the *"Annotationes"* of Valla in an old monastery. Thereafter the influence of Valla never left Erasmus. In the field of philology Valla was as much an influence and an ideal as Jerome was in the field of *bonae litterae* and the *philosophia Christi*. From the moment that Erasmus read the *"Annotationes"* of Valla the seeds were sown for Erasmus to do the same type of critical study as Valla had attempted almost a century before. But not only did Erasmus wish the same type of work for himself, he liked Valla's *Annotationes* so well that he published them himself with a well-worded dedicatory epistle [3] that defended the work and promulgated Valla's ideas even as he would his own.

The introductory epistle to the *Annotationes* of Valla presents a first-hand view of Erasmus' full commitment to the philological method:

"Neither am I of the opinion that theology, the queen of all disciplines, would be indignant if she is waited on and attended by her servant or handmaid, grammar; that although it follows in dignity, performs a large work that is necessary ... What if they reply that theology is too great to be directed by the laws of grammar, and that all work of interpretation is handed down by the inspiration of the Holy Spirit, it is

2) Ibid., 23.73. "Vt autem ad Italos veniam, quid Laurentia Vallensi, quid Philelpho veteris eloquentiae observantius?"
3) Ibid., 182. To Christopher Fisher.

certainly a new dignity for theologians, if they alone are able to speak incorrectly. But meanwhile let them explain what Jerome means when he writes to Desiderius that it is one thing to be a prophet and another to be an interpreter. In one instant the Spirit predicts and in the other words and sentences are intelligently conveyed by erudition ... For truly should we refer our errors to the authority of the Spirit? Even if the interpreters translated well, yet good translations can be perverted. Jerome emended, but his emendation is again depraved. Unless there is now less audacity among the semi-learned, or more skill of languages, or is it not easier to make mistakes by printing, which propogates a single error a thousand times" [4].

In this letter are already all the elements that Erasmus so well utilized in his own working with the text: erudition, eloquence, grammatical study, language study, correction, emendation, translation, critical appraisal, in short, a well-educated and learned scientific approach based upon the principle of philology. It is, as J. B. Pineau has pointed out, "une révision de la théologie" [5].

Valla indeed opened Erasmus' eyes to the philological method and Erasmus, with his genius pointing very definitely in the same direction, was able to utilize and perfect this method. From the time Erasmus came in contact with the "Annotationes" of Valla, he made up his mind that philology was the key to interpretation and he was never to change his views.

Erasmus' primary aim in life was the restoration of theology and he saw philology as the method by which he could bring this into being. Philology, therefore, played a dual role for Erasmus. Firstly, it presented to him the key to interpretation of the text, notably

---

4) Ibid., 182.132. "Ac ne ipsa quidem, opinor, disciplinarum omnium regina theologia ducet indignum admoueri sibi manus, ac debitum exhiberi obsequium a pedissequa grammatica; quae tametsi nonnullis est dignitate posterior, nullius certe opera magis necessaria ... (137) Quod si reclament maiorem esse theologiam quam vt grammaticae legibus teneatur, totum interpretandi negocium de sacri Spiritus afflatu pendere; nova vero theologorum dignitas, si solus illis licit barbare loqui. Sed expediant interim quid sibi velit, quod Desyderio suo scribit Hieronymus, aliud est, inquiens, esse vatem et aliud interpretem. Ibi Spiritus ventura praedicit; hic eruditio et verborum copia quae intelligit transferit. (151) Verum num etiam nostros errores ad Spiritum authorem referemus? Esto bene verterint interpretes; sed bene versa peruertuntur. Emendauit Hieronymus; at rursam deprauantur emendata. Nisi forte nunc aut minor audacia semidoctorum, aut peritia linguarum maior, aut non facillima deprauatio propter artem calchographicam, quae vnicum mendum repente in mille propagat exemplaria."

5) J. B. Pineau, *Èrasme, sa Pensée Religieuse*. Paris, 1924. p. 137.

the Holy Scriptures; and secondly, it presented to him the method by which he could restore the New Testament and the other texts that he felt would do the most to bring the Fathers back to a prime place of importance in theology [6].

As early as 1501, Erasmus saw that the *senus litteralis* of the Sacred Scriptures was dependent upon a good philological foundation. To Antony, Abbot of St. Bertin, Erasmus wrote,

> "I see it as madness to touch with the littlest finger that principal part of theology, which treats of divine mysteries, without first being instructed in Greek, when those who have translated the sacred books have in their scrupulous interpretation so rendered the Greek phrases that even the primary meaning which our theologians call 'literal' cannot be understood by those who do not know Greek" [7].

In this statement Erasmus is not only finding fault with the Scholastic theologians of his Paris days, but moreover he is beginning to see that philology is necessary in determining the literal sense of the Scriptures. Erasmus is laying here the groundwork for his fight to restore the New Testament text, and he is beginning his fight for a philological critical approach to the Scriptures. The more Erasmus learns and the more he tries to put his critical approach into practice, the more he will be attacked and the harder he will fight for these principles of Biblical criticism as a means to a better understanding of the *sensus litteralis*.

It is this humanistic interest in the philological critical method as a means to understanding the literal sense of the Scriptures that has caused Gerhard Ebeling to remark,

> "Durch Pflege der biblischen Sprachen, Texteditionen, saubere philologische Kommentierung und Ansätze zu kritischen Beobachtungen wurde dem *sensus litteralis* eine ungeahnte philologische Sorgfalt gewidmet" [8].

---

6) Erasmus edited editions of both the Latin and Greek Fathers — Ambrose, Athanasius, Augustine, Basil, Cyprian, Jerome, Hilary, Irenaeus, Chrysostom and was working on Origen when he died.

7) Allen, 149.21. "Video dementiam esse extremam, theologiae partem quae de mysteriis est praecipua digitulo attingere, nisi quis Graecanica etiam sit instructus supellectile, cum ii qui diuinos vertere libros, religione transferendi ita Graecas reddunt figuras, vt ne primarius quidem ille, quem nostrates theologi literalem nominant, sensus percipiatur ab iis que Graece nesciunt."

8) Gerhard Ebeling, *Die Religion in Geschichte und Gegenwart.* vol. III, "Hermeneutik", p. 250—1.

This deep-felt interest in the *sensus litteralis* led and prompted Erasmus to his editions of the New Testament. Erasmus saw that the New Testament edition that was available was far from being a correct and critical edition and it was his aim to bring forth an edition that was as perfect as possible, in both Greek and Latin, thereby giving Biblical scholars the opportunity to work toward the literal sense of the Scriptures. The method that Erasmus utilized to accomplish this was, of course, the philological critical method.

In his *Apologia* to *In Novum Testamentum Praefationes,* Erasmus states his method when he says that he wishes only to restore the New Testament to its correct form, replacing only that which has been distorted by the defects of time and the copyist, or that which is ambiguously rendered. He did not do this lightly nor leave anything to chance, for he primarily consulted the Canons, and he faithfully explained the examples of the Latin to the Greek original ... Laurentius Valla used only seven manuscripts while doing his work, but Erasmus used even more, one of which was a very old and pure Latin manuscript. But even then he was not satisfied, so he discussed and explored the tested authors so that he could make further observations, what they had quoted, what they had read, how they emended, how they interpreted. After all of this, Erasmus, with much care and vigilance, comparison and reflection, followed what he judged best, feeling that if a person has faith, the authority of the Holy Scriptures is not called into doubt, and if the Scriptures vary one should know this fact, that for over one thousand years neither the Latin nor the Greek manuscripts are of the same consensus. There had been carelessness, accidents, mistakes from lack of erudition, erasures, etc., that made these manuscripts vary ... Jerome in several places also noted this fact [9].

---

9) Holborn, 165.31. "Tantum restituimus, quae temporum ac librariorum vitio fuerant depravata, obiter indicatis et his, quae vel ambigue vel parum attente reddidit interpres (nam non recte mihi religio est dicere, etiamsi id non veritus est aliquot locis Hieronymus), idque fecimus neque levi quod dici solet brachio neque temere, sed primum ex canonum consilio, ad Graecae originis fidem examinatis exemplaribus Latinis, neque tamen fidentes paucis aut quibuslibet. Laurentius Valla septem bonae fidei codices se secutum fuisse testatur. Nos in prima recognitione quattuor Graecis adiuti sumus, in secunda quinque, in tertia praeter alia accessit editio Asculana, in quarta praesto fuit et Hispaniensis, deinde consultis tum pervetustis tum emendatis aliquot Latinae linguae voluminibus. Nec hoc contenti discussis et exploratis probatissimis auctoribus non oscitanter observavimus, quid citarint, quid legerint,

Erasmus follows with an apology for his own edition, saying that
Christians have always read Jerome, Cyprian, Hilary, Ambrose,
and Augustine. In these works one not only discovers differences,
but moreover contradictions. Also the Greek church has three
translations of the Septuagint. What are we to make of the fact
that none of these editions agree? And what of the commentaries
of men such as Bede, Thomas, and Lyra, all men of great intelli-
gence? Origen sees and explains the differences in the evangelical
writings. And then there are others that read Greek, others the
occidental writings. Moreover, around the time of Jerome some of
the Church followed the Septuagint while others accepted the new
translations from the Hebrew sources. And later some read the
Gallic church, some the Roman ... Certainly Augustine depended
upon the use of codices. But nevertheless all the ages stood firm
on the authority of their Scripture [10].

---

quid emendarint, quid interpretentur. Atque hisce rebus omnibus qua licuit
vigilantia, certe summa fide collatis ac pensitatis, quod optimum iudicavimus,
secuti sumus et hac lege in medium contulimus, ut nihilo secius suo quisque
iudicio frueretur. Iam vero si qui verentur, ne sacrarum litterarum auctoritas
vocetur in dubium, si quid usquam variaverit, hi sciant oportet iam annos
plus mille neque Latinorum neque Graecorum exemplaria per omnia consen-
sisse. Id quod ne fieri quidem possit, nimirum in tanta librariorum non solum
turba, verum etiam inscitia, oscitantia, temeritate. Ut ne commemorem, quam
multa mutata sint ab eruditulis aut certe a parum attentis. Comperio quaedam
erasa aut inducta a factionibus, quarum tumultu quondam sursum ac deorsum
miscebantur omnia, praesertim orientis ecclesiae, dum quisque pro suarum
partium patrocinio scripturam variat. Id certe factum non obscure compluribus in locis declarat Hieronymus."

10) Ibid., 166.28. "Quid autem accidit religioni Christianae, quod tot iam
saeculis aliud legit Hieronymus, aliud Cyprianus, aliud Hilarius, aliud Ambrosius, aliud Augustinus? Apud hos alicubi non modo diversa comperies,
sed et pugnantia, cum in summa Christianae fidei consentiant. Quid accidit
Graecis orthodoxis, qui sic secuti sunt translationem Septuaginta, ut subinde
meminerint Symmachi, Theodotionis et Aquilae? Quid facias, posteaquam nec
ipsa horum temporum edito per omnia sibi consentit? Qua de re si quis
dubitet, huic fidem fecerint codices typis etiam excusi cum annotamentis
marginalibus, quae declarant varietatem lectionis, et si id parum est, ex commentariis Bedae, Rabani, Thomae, ex commentariis Lyrani, ex commentariis
Hugonis Carensis idem intelliget. Origenes iam tum querebatur inexplicabilem
in euangelicis libris varietatem. Et publicitus aliud legit Graecia, aliud occi-
dentis ecclesia. Et circa aetatem Hieronymi quaedam ecclesiae sequebantur
interpretationem Septuaginta, quaedam novam amplectebantur ex Hebraeorum
fontibus traditam. Atque etiam post hanc aetatem aliud legebant Gallicanae
ecclesiae, aliud Romanae. Denique si excutias vetustos codices manu des-

Erasmus has presented a good historical argument showing that not only do the codices themselves vary, but the historical evidence shows that throughout the life of the Church there have been variations in both the writings of the revered Fathers and in the number of codices read and used by different persons. Erasmus then closes his apology by stating that in the light of all this overwhelming evidence he is not injuring the New Testament itself but rather he is restoring it by purifying, explaining, and amending it [11].

Of course, this apology did not change the minds of all the people to whom it was addressed, and Erasmus met quite a bit of opposition to his edition of the New Testament. Erasmus was well aware of this opposition. He had expressed his contempt for this type of radical conservatism in the *Moria* [12] and mocks this type of thinking in a letter to Wolfgang Fabricius Capito, saying that these conservatives see an end to faith in the Holy Scriptures if the text is amended [13].

He received a letter from Martin Dorpus, a professor in Louvain, challenging his edition of the New Testament, and Erasmus' answer not only presents more of an apology for his work, but it also gives more insights into his method.

In answering Dorpus, Erasmus naturally defends his edition of the New Testament, although this defense takes the form of an apologetical advocation of the philological critical method of text criticism. In this letter are all the elements that Erasmus thinks constitute a correct approach to scientific textual criticism. There is correction and emendation of the source; there is erudition; there

---

criptos, quibus in publico cultu tum utebantur, duos vix reperies inter se consentientes. Certe constat Augustinum codicibus usum, qui non vacabant mendis. Et tamen tot iam saeculis constitit sua scripturis auctoritas."

11) Ibid., 168.3. "Siquidem ea nostra castigatione non laeditur, sed redditur illustrior, purior, emendatior."

12) *Moria Encomiom,* LB iv, 470 c. "Negant enim e dignitate Sacrarum litterarum esse, si Grammaticorum legibus parere cogantur."

13) Allen, 541.83. "Nuper hic quidam apud plebem in sacra scilicet concione lachrymabili voce deplorauit actum esse de divinis literis ac theologis qui hoctenus fidem Christianam suis humeris fulsissent, posteaquam extitissent qui sacrosanctum Euangelium atque adeo ipsam orationem Dominicam emendarent: perinde quasi ego Matthaeum aut Lucam reprehendam, ac non eos potius quorum inscitia incuriaue deprauatum est quod illi recte scripserunt." Cf. ibid., 967.57. "His persuaderi non potest quin semel collapsura sit omnis ipsorum autoritas, si sacras libros habeamus emendatiores et horum intellectum ab ipsis petamus fontibus."

is analytical and comparative study of the meaning of the text through the utilization of the older theologians; and the outgrowth of this critical study is a text that Erasmus felt was accurate and better than anything else available in working toward the real and literal meaning of the Sacred Text itself.

> "I wonder what has happened with you that you turn your eyes from the investigation of the New Testament. You do not understand our aim when you say that we are trying to find fault with what so many centuries have approved ... What will you do when the Greek codexes read differently? Will you forget this and follow your codex, that perhaps is corrupted through a copyist ... Even a blind man can see that because of the lack of erudition of the interpreter or out of negligence the Greek text has been badly rendered, frequently even the true and genuine meaning is lost ... When this happens we run to Augustine, Ambrose, Hilary and Jerome. But only through going to the Greek source itself do we restore the true meaning. Laurentius Valla had few illustrations. Faber made only a commentary to the Pauline epistles, and gives the text in his own way. I have adapted the text after the Greek codices, and then I have included the Greek variants with all the comparisons. I have affixed separate annotations — sections that I have grounded on my own research, and sections with the authority of the ancient theologians, so that my corrections are not without ground ..." [14]

Such arguments as Dorpus' did not deter Erasmus from his determination to construct the New Testament text as accurately as possible, and in less than two years after his first edition of the

---

14) Ibid., 337.713. "Iam vero quod tertio loco scribis de Nouo Testamento, sane demiror quid tibi acciderit, aut quonam interim perspicacissimos ingenii tui oculos averteris. Nolis quicquam a me mutari, nisi, si quid forte sit apud Graecos significantius; et negas in hac qua vulgo vtimur aeditione quicquam esse vitii. Nefas esse putas rem tot saeculorum consensu, tot synodis approbatam, vllo pacto conuellere ... (730) At illud ipsa res clamitat et vel caeco, quod aiunt potest esse perspicuum, sepe vel ob imperitiam interpretis vel ob oscitantiam Graeca male reddita esse, sepe germanam ac veram lectionem ab indoctis librariis fuisse deprauatam, id quod cotidie videmus accidere, aliquoties mutatam a semidoctis parum attentis ... Et sunt fere eius modi quae mutamus, vt ad emphasim pertineant magis quam ad sensum ipsum; quanquam sepenumero magna sensus pars est emphasis. Verum non raro tota aberratum est via. Quod quoties accidit, quaeso te, quo confugit Augustinos, quo Ambrosius, quo Hilarius, quo Hieronymus, nisi ad Graecorum fontes? (859) Laurentius tantum annotauit locos aliquot, idque, vt apparet, in transcursu leuique, quod dici solet, brachio. Faber in Paulinas duntaxat Epistolas aedidit commentarios, easque suo more vertit: tum si quid discrepabat, obiter annotauit. Nos vniuersum Testamentum Nouum ad Graecorum exemplaria vertimus, additis e regione Graecis, quo cuiuis promptum

New Testament was published, he was busy at work on a new and better edition that was to be published in 1519. The fact is that instead of being worried over the attacks upon his first edition he was encouraged over the acclaim that the New Testament received and he was attempting to make more changes that he felt were needed.

> "Now what are they saying, that I am preparing a new edition because I am not satisfied with the former one — even if that is the case, what blame can they find? If I attempt to better myself, and do what was done by Origen, Jerome, and Augustine — especially since I had testified in my first edition that I had intended to do so if the occasion presented itself ... Besides this, where in my former translation I made very few changes for fear of offending less mature minds, I have now been exhorted by the advice of erudited men to venture a little further in that direction. I intend to support the changes made by more complete citation of the authorities so that those who are reluctant to believe may have no excuse" [15].

In another letter of this period, Erasmus writes to Antonia Pucci, the Roman legate to Switzerland, that his plans were to compare several Greek manuscripts, selecting the most genuine, translate this into Latin, and placing it by the side of the Greek text so that the reader might be able to compare the translation with the original. He also wished to preserve the integrity of the Latin language without doing harm to the simple Greek of the Apostles. Moreover, any passages which might give trouble to the reader, either because of ambiguity or obscurity or through faulty expression, would be explained and made clear with as little deviation as possible from the original words and no difference from the original meaning [16].

---

sit conferre. Adiecimus seperatim Annotationes, in quibus partim argumentis, partim veterum autoritate theologorum docemus non temere mutatum quod emendauimus, ne vel fide careat nostra correctio vel facile deprauari possit quod emendatum est."

15) Ibid., 809.56. "Iam quod cauillantur, ob id me parare nouam editionem quod prior mihi non satisfaciat, fingamus ita esse; quid est quod reprehendant? Si studeam meipso melior esse, et id facere quod ab Origene, quod ab Hieronymo factum est et ab Augustino? Praesertim cum id ingenue testatus sim in prima editione me facturum si foret vsus ... Ad haec, in translatione priore parcius mutaui, ne nimis offenderem istorum animos nimium morosos: nunc adhortantibus eruditis viris plusculum hac in parte sum ausus. Deinde locos immutatos crebriore autorum momenclatura communio, ne quid habeant quo tergiuersentur οἱ δυσπειθεῖς."

16) Ibid., 860.31. "Porro ne quis scrupulus habeat animum tuum, studii mei rationem paucis exponam. Collatis multis Graecorum exemplaribus, quod

Whether Erasmus is writing in the form of an apology or in explanation of his method concerning his editions of the New Testament the conclusions are the same: he is advocating and using a philological critical approach in his attempt to restore the New Testament text.

This philological method is rooted in the *fontes* and takes into consideration all the attainable texts [17], both codices and references in the Church Fathers, necessarily elevating the part of the grammarian to a place of prime importance in the field of hermeneutics.

In opposition to the prevalent thinking of his day, that felt that the task of interpretation rested solely on the shoulders of the theologians, Erasmus pointed out that some of the greatest and most revered of the Church Fathers were also grammarians. To Henry Bullock, Erasmus wrote:

> "Indeed it cannot be denied that Jerome, Ambrose, and Augustine, these men on whom our theological system mainly rests, belonged to the class of grammarians" [18].

Erasmus felt this grammatical principle was also rooted in the Scriptures themselves, for Paul had advocated the use of *sensus grammaticus* [19].

Erasmus thought that it was an error to attempt to deal with Holy Scriptures without a grammatical background and he saw the grammarians' place as a position of importance, second to none, in the matter of good textual criticism [20].

---

syncerissimum videbatur secuti, vertimus Latine, nostramque traductionem Graecis adiunximus, quo Lectori promptum sit conferre; et ita vertimus vt primum studuerimus, quoad licuit, integritati sermonis Romani, sed incolumi tamen Apostolici sermonis simplicitate. Deinde dedimus operam vt quae prius lectorem torquebant vel amphibologia vel obsuritate sermonis vel orationis vitiis aut incommodis, iam explanata sint ac dilucida; parcissime interim recedentes a verbis, a sensu nusquam."

17) K. A. Meissinger, *Erasmus von Rotterdam.* Zürich, 1942. p. 181. Meissinger states that with the new idea of a *"kritischen Textes auf Grund aller erreichbaren Textzeugen"*, and that *"Mit Erasmus beginnt die moderne Bibelkritik grossen Stils"*.

18) Allen, 456.137. "Neque negari potest Hieronymum, Ambrosium, Augustinum, quorum autoritate potissimum res theologica nititur, ex hoc grammaticorum ordine fuisse."

19) *Ecclesiastae,* LB v, 1044 a. "A Grammatico sensu, quemadmodum superius admonuimus, quam Paulus litteram appellat, recedere interdum cogit necessitas, interdum suadet utilitas."

With all this emphasis on the importance of the grammarian, yet in the *Moria* Erasmus can joke about people who attempt to become grammarians with only a scant knowledge of language. Erasmus points out that a little knowledge is a dangerous thing when he tells the story of a man who used the Hebrew letter שׁ, which is called *Schin* or *Sin*, and then showed how it meant *peccatum* (English *sin*) and from there moved to show that Jesus takes away the sin of the world [21].

In his more serious moments, such as in the *Apologia qua respondet duabus invectivis Eduardi Lei*, Erasmus does not hesitate to attribute or delegate to himself the position of grammarian or grammatician [22]. This is one issue on which Erasmus does not yield or hedge when under attack.

Erasmus knew that a grammarian would be occupied with details but he considered these details to be very important. For a man who has to collect, examine, handle, and interpret sacred literature must necessarily be occupied with details, but Erasmus saw that the details were not only important but one gained more information by working with these details [23].

Naturally the science of philology necessarily demands a knowledge of the original languages, particularly Greek, if one is working with the New Testament as Erasmus was. Erasmus' interest in Greek and his efforts in achieving accuracy in Greek have already been discussed in chapter one, so it is necessary only to point out here that Erasmus' attempt to deal with the Greek text of the New

---

20) Allen, 862.35. To Boniface Amorbach: "Atque illud protinus erat in promptu, Grammaticus est, non philosophus; rhetor est, non iureconsultus; orator est, non theologus."
Cf. ibid., 182.129. "... imo totum hoc, divinas vertere scripturas, grammatici videlicit partes sunt."
Cf. ibid., 1167.212. "Sunt qui me negant aliud esse quam grammaticum."

21) *Moria,* LB iv, 476 b. "Deinde docuit eam litteram apud Hebraias esse, שׁ, quam ille 'Syn' appellant: porro 'Syn' Scotorum, opinor, lingua, 'peccatum' sonat: atque hinc palam declarari, Jesum esse qui peccata tollerat mundi."

22) *Opuscula,* "Apologia ... Edvardi Lei", 1246. "In theologia nemo minus sibi sumpsit vnquam quam ego, qui partem omnium infimam, hoc est grammaticam, mihi delegerim, sublimiora illa relinquens felicioribus."

23) "Apologia", Holborn, 171.16. "Verum qui conferet, qui expendet, qui tractabit et interpretabitur sacras litteras, is ipse comperiet in his minutulis non minimum esse utilitatis."
Cf. Preface to the *Annotationes* (1515), Faber Tom. 6 a 2, LB vi, Allen, 373.111 ff, where Erasmus defends the importance of such *minutiae.*

Testament [24], rather than a translation, presents not only a different method from Scholastic exegesis, but it also played a tremendous part in basing the *sensus litteralis* on the original text rather than on a translation.

Naturally such a philological approach, with its grammatical and lingual interest, remolded exegesis, because such a method makes note of not one but several observations based on the information that is derived from this kind of literary and textual study [25].

The analytical reconstruction of the original text must be objective, therefore in a sense the Holy Scripture is to be interpreted as other books. The philological method, with its grammatical, literary, textual criticism, automatically leads toward an objective study. In his dedication of *Paraphrasis in Euangelium Ioannis*, Erasmus writes to Ferdinand, King of Austria, analyzing John's style:

> "Lastly John had his own peculiar style, so that he combines words in connecting phrases, sometimes from contraries, sometimes from similies, from time to time by repetition so that these paraphrases are unable to duplicate or restore the language. For example: '*In principio erat verbum, et verbum erat apud Deum, et Deus erat verbum!*' In this arrangement 'word' accompanies 'word'; 'God' accompanies 'God', then he repeats the beginning and completes the circle: *Hoc erat in principio apud Deum*. And again, *Omnia per ipsum facta sunt, et sine ipso factum est nihil. Quod factum est in ipso, vita erat, et vita erat lux hominum, et lux in tenebris lucat, et tenebrae eam non comprehenderunt*. It is apparent that the parts of speech always explain the former, so that the end of the former is the beginning of the following, and certainly you perceive that which the Greek ἠχώ customarily aims for, of which I have already spoken" [26].

---

24) Allen, 182.180. "Quorsum attinebat vt in Viennensi concilio tam sollicite statuerit authoritas ecclesiastica de parandis trium linguarum doctoribus?"

Cf. ibid., 149.42. "Sed quid ego e plurimis et maximis paucissima quaedam et leuicula repeto, cum mecum stet sacrosancta Pontificii senatus autoritas; cuius decretum extat adhuc in Epistolis Decretalibus, vt in praecipuis (vti tum erant) Academiis pararentur qui Hebraicas, Graecas, Latinasque literas perfecte possent tradere, quod sine his diuinas literas percipi posse negarent, multo autem minus tractari?"

25) *Ratio*, Holborn, 273.23. "Annotanda erit et verborum emphasis, quam ad rem plurimum conducit diversarum cognitio linguarum."

26) Allen, 1333.50. "Postremo habet Ioannes suum quoddam dicendi genus, ita sermonem velut ansulis ex sese cohaerentibus contexens; nonnunquam ex contrariis, nonnumquam ex similibus, nonnumquam ex iisdem subinde repetitis, vt paraphrasis has orationis delicias non possit reddere. Quod genus est: 'In principio erat verbum, et verbum erat apud Deum, et Deus erat

This philological critical method of interpretation also makes the Scriptures more approachable, more easily understood. The "dark spots" are easier to handle when one utilizes such an approach as Erasmus'. This is just another way of saying that the philological critical method is a tremendous asset to the cause of erudition, for this approach presents an erudite and objective attempt to deal with the interpretation of Scripture.

The philological critical approach of Erasmus places considerable emphasis on the analytical value of comparisons. As Erasmus states in the title of his edition of the New Testament, this use of comparisons encompasses the analyzing and comparing of the manuscripts, both Latin and Greek, and at the same time utilizing and comparing the proven authorities on the subject matter [27].

In his desire for excellence Erasmus places a great deal of importance on the readings of the Church Fathers, comparing them in order to obtain a better reading of the passage, and stating their views so that the reader can get the benefit of their views, even though, as Erasmus states, sometimes even they are mistaken. To Henry Bullock Erasmus writes,

> "Now in the first place I do not alter all parts (of the New Testament), for the most important places remain unchanged, yet I show the places where the discrepancies exist. I reveal that in some instances Hilary was mistaken, also Augustine and Aquinas . . ." [28]

In his letter to Pope Leo X, Erasmus is not so matter of fact as he presents his comparative method, yet the emphasis on the importance of comparing the manuscripts and the Fathers is central:

> "For by this labor we do not intend to weaken the old and commonly received edition, but to emend it where it is depraved, and to illustrate

---

verbum.' In his tribus membris, verbum verbo, Deus Deo succinitur, ac mox repititio principio circulum absoluit: 'Hoc erat in principio apud Deum.' Ac rursum: 'Omnia per ipsum facta sunt, et sine ipso factum est nihil. Quod factum est in ipso, vita erat, et vita erat lux hominum, et lux in tenebris lucet, et tenebrae eam non comprehenderunt.' In his liquet vt orationis quodque membrum semper excipiat prius, sic ut prioris finis sit initium sequentis, ac tale quiddam hic agnoscas, quale Graecorum ἠχώ solet affectare, quibus de rebus nonnihil dictum est nobis in argumentis."

27) LB vi, 1—2. "Novum Testamentum juxta Graecorum lectionem ex emendatioribus exemplaribus ex veterum Orthodoxorum lectione, cum versione Desiderii Erasmi Roterodami."

28) Allen, 456.114. "Principio nec passim muto, nam summe constat: de locis modo aliquot disceptatio est . . . Ostendo locis aliquot lapsum esse Hilarium, lapsum Augustinum, lapsum Thoman . . ."

where it is obscure; and not by the dreams of my own mind, nor as they say, with unwashed hands, but partly by the evidence of the early codices, and partly by the opinions of those whose learning and sanctity have been approved by the authority of the Church. I mean Jerome, Hilary, Ambrose, Augustine, Chrysostom, and Cyril: Meanwhile we are always prepared to give our reasons for anything which we have rightly taught, or to correct with pleasure any passage where we as men have fallen into error" [29].

Through this extensive use of comparison Erasmus was able to select the word or phrase that best conveyed his desired meaning. This type of work demanded an extra thoroughness, which was made to order for Erasmus since it was in this field that his interest lay, and it was to this type of philological work that Erasmus was to devote a great deal of his life.

Erasmus' annotations to the New Testament sometime amount to little more than a comparative study, since he points out the reading that he prefers from the Greek manuscripts, comparing it with the Vulgate and then noting how certain of the Fathers agree, or, in certain instances, disagree with the Greek manuscripts.

Erasmus shows his dependence upon this philological critical comparative study when he writes preceding his second edition of the New Testament:

"However we do not rely on our dreams, but we seek the readings of Origen, Basil, Chrysostom, Cyril, Jerome, Cyprian, Ambrose, and Augustine ... always upon the judgments of the old authors. We do not weaken or destroy this edition of the Vulgate, which however is of doubtful authorship ... If it is desirable that we have the Divine Writings most correct, this labor of mine not only corrects the errors of the Sacred Volumes, but helps to prevent mistakes in the future ... Though we have translated the Greek readings we still do not approve it everywhere: in some places we prefer our own text, always indicating where the orthodox Latin writers agree or disagree with the Greek. Further, the variety of the readings not only does not hinder the study of the Sacred Scriptures but it is conducive to that study, according to

---

29) Ibid., 446.59. "Nec enim hoc labore veterem ac vulgo receptam aeditionem conuellimus, sed alicubi deprauatam emendamus, aliquot locis obscuram illustramus; idque non ex anima mei somniis nec illotis, vt aiunt, manibus, sed partim ex vetustissimorum codicum testimoniis, partim ex eorum sententia quorum et doctrinam et sanctimoniam ecclesiastica comprobauit autoritas, nempe Hieronymi, Hillarii, Ambrosii, Augustini, Chrysostomi, Cyrilli: semper interim parati aut modeste rationen reddere si quid recte docuimus, aut libenter corrigere sicubi imprudentes, vt homines, lapsi sumus."

Saint Augustine. Neither is the variety so important as to lead to the peril of the orthodox faith" [30].

The philological critical method includes many facets: textual and literary criticism, grammatical study, attention to details, superior knowledge of the original languages, the use of comparisons — both of the texts and commentaries, corrections, emendations, citing of authors, interpretations, and annotations. Of course, many of these overlap, but nevertheless they are all valuable tools of the philologist. Erasmus utilized all of the above and in the light of his times, it can be said, he utilized them with immense success.

In the preceding sections we have shown Erasmus' method as he himself has stated it in his writings and letters. We have tried as far as possible to let Erasmus speak and explain his principle of interpretation and the approach that he uses. We feel that we have not been far from wrong in stating that Erasmus sees the philological critical method as the key to unlocking the literal meaning of the *fontes*, and for this reason Erasmus uses philology as the method of interpretation.

So far we have only developed Erasmus' hermeneutic. Now let us turn our attention to how Erasmus applies these hermeneutical principles to the New Testament, to the application that Erasmus derives from his principles of interpretation.

As we view the crowning accomplishment of Erasmus, *In Novum Testamentum cum Annotationes*, we must not forget the principle that was stated earlier. Erasmus was an innovator and he attempted something new in his editions of the New Testament. Like all forerunners, the men who came after have the advantage, for they can profit by the former's mistakes. It is not our task to judge, but to present. A presentation compels a type of evaluation, but in an

---

30) Ibid., 860.40. "Quem tamen non ex nobisipsis somniamus, sed ex Origene, Basilio, Chrysostomo, Cyrillo, Hieronymo, Cypriano, Ambrosio, Augustino, petimus ... semper veterum autorum nixi sententia. Vulgatam hanc aeditionem non conuellimus — quae tamen cuius sit incertum est ... Si optandum est vt diuinos habeamus quam emendatissimos, hic meus labor non solum amolitur mendas sacrorum voluminum, verumetiam obstat ne posthac queant deprauari ... Graecorum lectionem licet vbique verterimus, non tamen vbique probamus: quin nostram alicubi praeferimus, semper indicantes vbi scriptores oxthodoxi Latini cum Graecis consentiant aut dissentiant. Porro lectionis varietas non solum non officit studio sacrarum Scripturarum verumetiam conducit, autore diuo Augustino. Neque tamen vsquam tanta est varietas vt ad orthodoxae fidei periculum pertineat."

evaluation we can grasp the significance of Erasmus' method, while judgment only tends to blur the importance of Erasmus.

In his translation of John 1.1 [31], Erasmus uses the Latin word *sermo* instead of the normal translation of *verbum*, because he feels that *sermo*, which has the connotation of rational discourse, is a better word to express the Greek *logos* concept. Here Erasmus carefully explains the meaning of the Greek *logos*. He, to be sure, took this concept in its classical meaning, but the important point for our investigation is that he attempted to find a Latin word that would most clearly convey the Greek concept of *logos*. This is the reason that he chose *sermo* over *verbum*, for it more clearly fitted what Erasmus felt the *lógos* concept should convey [32]. Had Erasmus known Koine Greek he would no doubt have rendered *logos* differently.

This brings us to Erasmus' Greek style, which was built entirely on classical Greek, without any benefit of the knowledge of Koine or the vernacular Greek that was in common usage during the period of the writing of the New Testament. But, although Erasmus continually follows the classical usage in the opening lines of the *Annotationes*, he nevertheless deviates from his accepted policy in explaining the meaning of the Greek word *evangelion*, εὐαγγέλιον. He gives Homer's usage of the term, and adds that in the Gospels it means 'good announcements' and that Christ and the Apostles gave to the word a new meaning [33].

Erasmus' exactness in grammatical detail led him to some different translations. In John 16.13, he translates ὁδηγήσει as *ducet vos in omnia veritatem*, while the Vulgate translates this *docebit* [34]. In Acts 18.16, Erasmus translates ἀπήλασεν as *et abegit eos* while the Vulgate reads *et minavit eos* [35]. In Romans 5.12, the Greek reads

---

31) LB vi, 336. cf. ibid., 1082, in which the third edition uses *sermo* to translate the λόγος of 1 John 5.7, the famous *Comma Ioanneum* that he reinserted in this edition.

32) See *Apologia de 'in principio erat sermo'*, LB ix, 111—122.

33) Ibid., vi 1. "Εὐαγγέλιον graece sonat bonum nuncium. Quamquam Homerus in Odyssia hoc verbo est usus pro praemio quod dari dari laetum adferenti nuncium. Igitur historiam evangelicam nec prophetiam vocavit, nec aliud simile, sed rem novam novo vocabulo signavit, quemadmodum et Christus apostolis vocabulum innovaret."

34) Ibid., 404. The *Annotationes* adds "Graece non est docebit, sed ducet, ὁδηγήσει, et in omnem veritatem."

35) Ibid., 505—506.

ἐφ' ᾧ πάντες ἥμαρτον and Erasmus translates this as *et sic omnes homines mors pervasit* over against the Vulgate, *in quo omnes peccaverunt* [36]. In I Timoty 3.16, Erasmus' reading is *magnum est pietatis mysterium:* Deus (Θεός for ὅς) *manifestatus est in carne* while the Vulgate is *magnum est pietatis sacramentum, quod manifestatum est in carne* [37]. For ἐξ ἀκοῆς πίστεως in Galatians 3.2, Erasmus has *ex praedictione fidei*, understanding ἀκοή as meaning 'instruction' rather than 'hearing' as the Vulgate does with its rendering of this phrase by the Latin *ex auditu fidei* [38]. On the controversial meaning of Paul in Galatians 6.11, ῎Ιδετε πηλίκοις ὑμῖν γράμμασιν ἔγραψα, Erasmus understands this to mean *videtis quanta vobis epistola scripserim*, while the Vulgate reads, *videte qualibus litteris scripsi vobis* [39].

In the first edition of the New Testament the Greek codex for Revelation 22.16—21 was missing, so, to the detriment of theology and the field of Bible interpretation, Erasmus retranslated this into Greek from his Latin Bible and codices, with the exception of verse twenty, which he borrowed from Valla's annotations. However, in the third edition the Greek text approximates the present edition, except in verse 16: ὀρθρινός instead of Πρωινός. Verse 17: ἐλθέ twice for ἔρχου; and ἐλθέτω for ἐρχέσθω. Verse 18 differs greatly from the Nestle text. Verse 19: βίβλῳ in place of ξύλου; addition of articles, and difference in word forms. Verse 20: an extra 'Αμὴν and ναί. Verse 21: the addition of ἡμῶν and Χριστοῦ and ὑμῶν, and in closing with 'Αμήν [40].

The editions of the New Testament with their annotations illustrates the philological interest of Erasmus, and in most instances when theological questions do arise they are treated in a philological manner. In Matthew 3.2, Erasmus translates μετανοεῖτε by *poenitentiam agite*, and he proposes that it could also mean *resipiscite* (to be mindful) or *ad mentum redite* (come to yourselves) [41].

In dealing with Romans 1.17, the passage that meant so much to Luther, Erasmus sees the theological significance as of minor importance. Erasmus' interest is in comparing this verse with the reading

---

36) Ibid., 583—585.
37) Ibid., 935—936.
38) Ibid., 813—814.
39) Ibid., 827—828.
40) Ibid., 1123—1125.
41) Ibid., 17—18.

of Habakkuk 2.4, Galatians, and James, and the various renderings of the meaning of ἐκ πίστεως ζήσεται [42].

In an argument with Lefèvre over the correct meaning of the expression καὶ μετὰ τρεῖς ἡμέρας ἀναστήσεται in Mark 10.34, Erasmus says that the problem can be cleared up by understanding this as a figure of speech. Lefèvre had said it was inconsistent to say one arose after the third day, when in fact he arose the third day. Erasmus answers that this is not the case if we understand the meaning of 'after the third day he arose' as 'he arose to appear after the third day' [43].

Though Erasmus' interest is not primarily theological, he utilized the philological method to make theological points. He pointed out that the Vulgate reading of Psalm 50.4 was not correct. His theological point was that the Greek, instead of meaning *peccatum meum contra me est semper* (Vulgate), meant *sed semper veluti praesens obuersaretur* [44].

There is one philological mistake that Erasmus made that was carried over to the King James English translation of the Bible, one that was theologically unsound. This concerns the statement in Luke 2.14. Erasmus said the Greek text should read ἀνθρώποις εὐδοκία, Latin *hominibus bona voluntas* (good will toward men), while the Vulgate read *hominibus bonae voluntatis* [45]. Nestle reads

---

42) Ibid., 561—564.

43) Allen, 778.216. "Cum vnica synecdoche res omnis potuerit expedire, si intelligamus post tres dies resurrexisse qui post tercium diem exortum surrexerit? Faber enim imaginatur nullo pacto consistere vt dicatur post tercium diem surrexisse qui tercio die surrexerit." Of course this argument arose over the difference of the Greek text and the Apostles' and Nicene Creeds. Erasmus appears to have received so much criticism over his translation 'after the third day' that in the third edition of his New Testament he translates it *et tertia die resurget* (LB vi, 192), as the Vulgate does, thereby alleviating the difficulty of agreement with the creeds. However it is interesting that in the above quoted letter Erasmus attempts to derive the theological meaning through the use of grammatical principles that allow him to, as he saw it, remain true to the Greek text.

44) Ibid., 149.26. "Quis enim illud in Psalmo intelligat, Et peccatum meum contra est semper, nisi Graeca legerit? qua sunt huiusmodi, καὶ ἡ ἁμαρτία μου ἐνώπιόν μου ἐστὶ διαπαντός. Hic mihi theologus quispiam longam texuerit fabulam quomodo caro cum spiritu pugnet assidue, praepositionis, scilicet contra, deceptus amphibologia, cumillus ἐνώπιον non pugnam sed situm significet, perinde ac si dices, e regione, id est in conspectu: vt significarit Propheta culpam suam vsqueadeo sibi displicere, vt eius memoria nunquam ab animo recederet, sed semper veluti praesens obuersaretur."

ἀνθϱώποις εὐδοχίας. So both Nestle and the Vulgate agree that the meaning is 'to men of good will'. This is one place that it would have been better if Erasmus had let the traditional meaning stand.

Erasmus did a great service both to Biblical criticism and theology in his first two editions of the New Testament when he omitted the famous *Comma Ioannum* of 1 John 5.7,8. He reinserted this in his third edition when a supposedly very ancient Greek manuscript was presented to him that contained this controversial passage [46].

When Erasmus translates the Greek word ἐϰϰλησία according to its context rather than literally, he is using the philological historical critical method in order to derive the best meaning from the Greek. It is in cases such as this that this method pays off, for it leads to a better theological understanding of the passage, particularly if we consider that the great majority of the men who read his New Testament were unfamiliar with the Greek.

In the passage relating to the near riot of the people in the giant theatre at Ephesus in Acts 19.32,40 [47], Erasmus uses *concio* (assembly) rather than *ecclesia*. But where ἐϰϰλησία has references to a gathering of the Church in Acts 5.11; 7.38; 11.22,26; 14.27 [48]; Romans 16.5 [49]; 2 Corinthians 1.1 [50]; Philemon 1.2 [51]; 3 John 1.10 [52]; Erasmus uses *congregatio*, from which the English word 'congregation' is derived [53].

Yet Erasmus' emphasis on philology caused him to fail to grasp certain theological truths for in translating the Greek σωτήϱ Erasmus uses *servator* (preserver) rather than the Vulgate *salvator* (savior) [54].

---

45) LB vi, 231—34.
46) Ibid., 1079—81.
47) Ibid., 509—10.
48) Ibid., 455—6; 463—4; 479—80; 590—1.
49) Ibid., 651—52.
50) Ibid., 751—52.
51) Ibid., 977—78.
52) Ibid., 1087—88.
53) In the book of Acts where the word ἐϰϰλησία is used more than any other book, Erasmus translates it *ecclesia* in all but 7 times: *5-congregatio, 2-concio.*
54) LB vi. Lu 1.47 (226); 2.11 (232); Jn 4.32 (358); Acts 5.31 (458); 13.23 (986); Phl 3.20 (876); I Tim 1.1 (916); 4.10 (938); 2 Tim 2.10 (952); 2 Pet 1.1 (1058); 1.11 (1060); I Jn 4.14 (1078); Jud 1.25 (1092).

In the *Annotationes*, when writing on 1 Timothy 3.16, Erasmus forgets his philological principles completely in order to speak theologically. This is rather an interesting illustration, for it is so different from the normal Erasmian approach that it is refreshing to see reflections of this nature by Erasmus. Erasmus thought that the noun θεός should be read in place of the Greek relative pronoun ὅς, thereby strengthening the meaning in order to combat the Arian heresy [55].

When Erasmus' philological criticism is not based on grammatical principles as the illustrations on the preceding pages pointed out, then it is based on the use of comparisons. It is this reliance on comparisons that Erasmus utilized to such a great extent that ties him so closely to his principle of *eruditio*, but moreover it is an attempt on Erasmus' part to take into consideration all the available material, both textual and exegetical, on any given verse in order to give the best possible reading on that verse.

In his annotation on Romans 5.12, Erasmus goes into a lengthy discussion over the meaning of the verse, utilizing several of the Fathers to help him derive the proper explanation. He shows that Origen, Ambrose, and Augustine have given the passage a twofold meaning in trying to explain it, and after giving their positions, Erasmus discusses the use of Scripture against heresies, concluding that in fighting with one's opponents one must not distort the sacred writings in order to gain a victory, as some of the Fathers did [56].

Erasmus' notes are usually not so long and theological as those found in the fifth chapter of Romans, where Paul is dealing with the doctrine of original sin, in which, Erasmus feels, the passages need some type of explanation along with a presentation and comparisons with the earlier theologians. In most instances the notes only explain why Erasmus translates a particular word or phrase the way he does.

The use of comparisons by Erasmus normally takes two forms. One is the method of explanation, either theological as in the preceding illustration, or by way of simple explanation as to the meaning of the term. The other is the use of comparisons in order to show the best rendering of the word, phrase, or verse by taking

---

55) Ibid., 935.938.
56) Ibid., 584—90.

into consideration all the available readings on the text, either Greek and Latin manuscripts or the renderings of the Fathers on the subject.

An example of the simple explanation Erasmus uses can be found in the annotations as early as Matthew 1.16, where Erasmus explains the meaning of the Greek preposition ἐκ by comparing the use of the Latin prepositions *ex* and *de*[57].

To illustrate briefly the second point, in Romans 5.16, Erasmus says that the Greek reading is obscure, so he compares the reading of the Vulgate, one Latin Father — Ambrose, and one Greek Father — Chrysostom[58]. In Romans 12.13, in order to find the best rendering of ταῖς χρείαις τῶν ἁγίων κοινωνοῦντες, Erasmus gives Ambrose's Latin translation *(memoriis)*, but then he gives the reading of Chrysostom and Theophylaactus, pointing out that their reading, χρείαις, must be translated as *necessitatibus*, which is the reading that he gives to the phrase[59].

Though showing preference for the reading of the Fathers, both Latin and Greek, Erasmus will nevertheless use classic authors[60] and the scholastic interpreters[61] in his comparative study when he thinks that they help to illustrate or explain the meaning of a passage.

In his editions of the New Testament, Erasmus brought to the Scriptures for the first time a real scientific text criticism. In his philological critical approach, Erasmus promoted a science that was to have a profound effect on the method of exegesis of Scripture.

This philological critical method that Erasmus did so much to promote, with its attempt to discover the original and literal meaning of the text, was an aid to the early exegesis of Luther. In the *Scholia* of his early expositions of Scripture, Luther is at times very philological-grammatical in character.

In chapter one we saw that Luther, in contrast to Erasmus, kept the medieval formula of exegesis, with its *glossa* and *scholia*,

---

57) Ibid., 3—4.

58) Ibid., 591—2. "Apud Graecos obscurius est ..."

59) Ibid., 632. "*necessitatibus sanctorum communicantis.* Ambrosius (Memoriis), Chrysostomus et Theophylactus (χρείαις), id is *Necessitatibus.*"

60) In the *Annotationes* on εὐαγγέλιον (LB vi, 1) and μετανοεῖτε (LB vi, 17—8) Erasmus quotes Homer's usage of these two words.

61) Ibid., 17—18. For instance in his notes on Matthew 3.4, Erasmus quotes Rabanas and Lyra along with the Ancients.

and that Luther quoted extensively from the Middle Age writers. But Luther also utilized the latest methods of exegesis, particularly the philological method. He used Erasmus' editions of the New Testament, particularly in his early exegetical works, namely the *Römerbriefvorlesung* (1515—6), the *Galaterbriefvorlesung* (1516 —7), and the *Hebräerbriefvorlesung* (1517—8). In reviewing excerpts from these it will become clear how much Luther utilized both the New Testament of Erasmus and the philological critical method. It will also illustrate both the similarities and differences of the exegetical method of Luther and Erasmus.

Novum Instrumentum omnia cum Annotationibus was published in Basel in late February, 1516, and beginning with the ninth chapter of his *Römerbriefvorlesung*, Luther used it extensively as reference material.

Luther follows Erasmus' translation in Romans 9.15. "The Greek text reads: 'I will have mercy on whom I will have mercy and I will have compassion on whom I will have compassion'" [62]. In Romans 9.10, Luther prefers the Vulgate reading, *patris nostri*, which Erasmus had translated *patre nostro* [63]. Luther follows Erasmus when he says in Romans 9.19, "This is why the Greek text does not say as ours does: 'Who are you that you reply to him?' but 'that you reply against' or 'in opposition to him'" [64]. In discussing Romans 10.12, Luther follows Erasmus' translation of "noemata" in Philippians 4.7: "In the same way he says in Philippians: 'And the peace of God that surpasses all thought' (noun), i. e., knowing, feeling, and as we said before, 'keep your hearts and minds', i. e., 'noemata', i. e., that you feel and think by reason and mind, or as they would say, 'your thoughts'" [65]. Luther says that in

---

62) WA, 56.397.7. "Graecus sic: 'Miserebor, cuiuscunque misereor, et commiserabor, quemcunque commiseror', . . ."
Cf. Erasmus, LB vi, 614. Romans 9.15 "Miserebor cujuscumque misereor, et commiserabor quemcumque commiseror."

63) WA, 56.395.10. cf. Erasmus, LB vi, 612. Romans 9.10.

64) Ibid., 56.401.4. "Ideo in Greco habetur non, ut nos habemus, 'qui respondeas', sed 'qui contra' seu 'adversus respondes', . . ."
Cf. Erasmus, LB vi, 614. Romans 9.19.

65) WA, 56.421.10. "Eodem modo dicit Phil.: 'Et pax Dei, que exuperat omnem sensum' (i. e. 'Noyn'), hoc est sapere, sentire intelligere, ut supra, 'custodiat corda vestra et sensus vestros' i. e. 'Noemata', hoc est sensa et mentata per mentem vel sensum, ubi nos 'intelligentias vestras'."
Cf. Erasmus, LB vi, 876. Phil. 4.7.

Romans 11.4 "Bezebub" means "lord of the flies" *(vir muscarum)* and "Beelphogor" means "lord of the corpse". Erasmus translated these *cadaveris* and *muscarum idolum* [66]. Luther says that in Romans 11.9 "trap" in this context can mean "deception" or better, "hunt", *(venatu)*, following Erasmus' *venatus* [67]. Luther and Erasmus both translate the phrase in Romans 11.13, "I will glorify my ministry" by *glorificio* instead of the Vulgate *honorificabo* [68]. In translating the "first fruits" of Romans 11.16, both Lefèvre and Erasmus have *primitiae*, but Luther has *primitie* [69]. In discussing Romans 11.20, Luther excerpts the phrase, "It has reference to inward disposition rather than to the intellect" *(Ideo magis refertur ad affectum quam ad intellectum)*, from Erasmus' annotation to Romans 11.25 *(magis ad affectum regertur quam ad prudentiam)* [70]. Luther says of Romans 11.29 that the Greek text reads "God's gifts are irreversible *(amitameliata,* i. e., *impenitibilia)* Erasmus reads *impoenitibilia* [71].

This extensive use by Luther of Erasmus' translation and annotations decreases following the eleventh chapter of Romans. However Luther continues to make use of Erasmus' work even though he no longer is as dependent on it as he is in chapters 9—11. In discussing the phrase in Romans 13.13, "not in reveling and drunkenness", Luther says that the Greek word "comos" is the Greek god of intoxication [72]. In his notes on Romans 15.20 (and I have preached the gospel), Luther says that the Greek says, "I have been ambitious to preach the gospel" *(Sic autem ambitiosus fui praedicare evangelium)*. Erasmus' translation of this verse reads *ita annitens*

---

66) WA, 56.430.13. "Inde 'Beelzebub' i. e. 'vir muscarum' ac 'Beelphogor' i. e. 'vir cadaveris'."
Cf. LB vi, 622. Romans 11.4.

67) WA, 56.432.17. "'Captio' autem hoc loco pro 'decipula' potest accipi, sed aptius pro 'venatu', qua captione fere capiuntur."
Cf. Erasmus, LB vi, 622. Romans 11.9.

68) WA, 56.434.8. cf. Erasmus, LB vi, 624. Romans 11.13.

69) WA, 56.435.4. cf. Erasmus, LB vi, 624. Romans 11.16.

70) WA, 56.435.20. cf. Erasmus, LB vi, 625. Romans 11.25.

71) WA, 56.440.6. cf. Erasmus, LB vi, 626. Romans 11.29.

72) WA, 56.488.10. "Sicut a 'Graecus' 'grecari', ita a 'Comos' 'comessari' videtur venire. Est autem 'Comos' Grece convivium, immo luxus convivii et effusus immoderatusque convivii apparatus seu usus."
Cf. Erasmus, LB vi, 638. Romans 13.13. "Comos autem Graecis deus est temulentiae."

praedicare evangelium and his note reads *veluti ambitiose conari quippiam*[73].

Luther's use of Erasmus in his *Galaterbrief* and *Hebräerbrief-vorlesung* is not so pronounced. Yet as the illustrations will point out, he still used Erasmus' translation and notes as an aid in getting to the heart of the text; although at the same time he shows he is not dependent on them. In Galatians 1.4 Luther quotes Luke 2.13, *"In terra pax, hominibus bona voluntas seu beneplacitum"*. As we noted on page 116, Erasmus translated this "hominibus bona voluntas", an obviously bad translation of the Greek[74]. In Galatians 1.10 both Luther and Erasmus use the word *hactenus*[75]. In discussing the word "bewitched" in Galatians 3.1 Luther says, *"'fascinare' dicitur, qui aspectu malefico ledit,* and Erasmus has *"'fascinare' dicuntur Latinis, qui aspectu malefico laedunt"*[76]. On the allegory of the two mountains in Galatians 4.24 ff, Luther says that he learned from Erasmus that 'mountain' is genitive neuter *(oros est generis neutri. Hoc ex Erasmo)*[77].

When exegeting Romans 12.16 Luther uses many grammatical distinctions of the meaning of *humile* that do not follow Erasmus' annotation on the same verse, but the thinking is in all likelihood derived from Erasmus[78]. When discussing Romans 10.15 (How beautiful are the feet of them that preach the gospel) Luther gained valuable knowledge from the annotation of Erasmus on this verse. Erasmus had stated that Paul was *iuxta veritatem hebraicam* in Isaiah 52.7, and then he pointed to the exegesis of Jerome. Luther states, "What is the meaning of 'feet'? According to a first inter-pretation, they signify the inner attitude of those who preach. But according to the Hebrew and a better exegesis ... it signifies the communication of the preaching, for voices are like feet in that

---

73) WA, 56.524.13. cf. Erasmus, LB vi, 648. Romans 15.20.

74) WA, 57.56.8.

75) Ibid., 58.12. cf. Erasmus, LB vi, 804. Gal. 1.10.

76) WA, 57.75.8. cf. Erasmus, LB vi, 811. Gal. 3.1.

77) WA, 57.97.3. cf. Erasmus, LB vi, 820. Gal. 4.24.

78) WA, 56.471.19. "Quod 'humile' nostra translatio promiscue accipit, cum in Greco aliud sit 'Tapinosis', 'Tapinos' i. e., 'humilitas', 'humilis' seu 'vilis', 'vilitas' propria significatione Latina, qua 'humilitas' dicitur contrarium sublimi seu nobili."

Cf. Erasmus, *Annotationes* on Romans 12.16 (LB vi, 633). "'Humiles' hic vocat non modestos, sed humilis fortis homines, veluti pauperes, ignobiles, indoctos, plebejos."

they convey the meaning to the ears of the hearer" [79]. In the *glossa* to Hebrews 17.3 Luther says 'through faith' means 'by faith' *(per fidem)*, as Erasmus translated it [80].

It is in Luther's discussion of Erasmus' translation and annotations that we really discern the difference between the exegesis of Luther and Erasmus. In the *scholia* on Romans 10.6 (Who shall ascend into heaven?) Luther says,

> "Erasmus sees no difficulty here and thinks that the expositors struggle in vain, because, in his opinion, the apostle means to say by these words that Moses wanted to curb those who do not believe unless they have direct evidence ... To one who does not believe this and says: 'Who shall ascend into heaven?' does the same as one who denies that Christ is there or who demands that he shall be given proof and evidence for his faith. However this may be, I think the apostle means to say that the righteousness of man leading to salvation depends on the word apprehended by faith and not a work based on knowledge" [81].

In discussing Romans 9.19 in his *scholia* Luther states:

> "Some, like Laurentius Valla, take this phrase to be passive, Lefèvre understands it as referring to a person, but Erasmus says all the Greek interpreters take it as deponent and he agrees with them ..." [82]

Concerning the Greek word 'analogia' in Romans 12.6, Luther had written in the *scholia:*

> "For some interpreters take the Greek word *analogia* to mean 'rule', 'compassion', 'proportion', 'similarity'. The apostle means that if one

---

79) WA, 56.424.11. "Quid autem per 'pedes'? Secundum primam acceptionem significat affectus et vota pradicantium, que debent esse syncera ab omni lucro et gloria. Sed secundum Hebreum et veriorem, ... verius tamen significant ipsa verba eorum seu sonum et syllabas, dictiones, verborum, pradicationem, quia voces sunt velut pedes et vehicula vel rote, quibus vehitur, volvitur aut graditur verbum ad aures auditorum." Cf. Erasmus, LB vi, 619. Romans 10.15.

80) WA, 57.62.4. cf. LB vi, 1012. Heb. 11.3.

81) WA, 56.415.15. "Erasmus putat hic nihil esse difficultatis et frustra laborari ab expositoribus, sc. quod Apostolus velit Mosen istis verbis eos compescuisse, qui non credunt, nisi experimentum rei videant, ut: 'Quis ascendet in celum?' i. e., nec dixeris: Christus non est in celis, licet non videas, sed tantum crede. Qui enim hoc non credit et dicit: 'Quis ascendit in celum?' hic idem facit, ut qui neget Christum illic esse aut velit sibi experimentum huius fidei fieri. Sed quicquid sit, intentio Apostoli est, quod tota iustitia hominis ad salutem pendet ex verbo per fidem et non ex opere per scientiam."

82) Ibid., 400.14. "Hoc aliqui passive, vt Laurentius Vallensis, Stapulensis personaliter, sed Erasmus dicit omnes interpretes grecos deponentaliter accipere, quibus ispe consentit."

wants to prophesy, prophesy in such a way that you do not exceed faith, so that your prophesying is in line with your faith. In German we say, 'Es ellicht ym gleich'."

Erasmus had translated this by *iuxa portionem fidei*, and in his annotations he has remarked *iuxta proportionem fidei* [83]. In his *scholia* on Romans 15.17 Luther states that others (Erasmus) are of the opinion that the apostle speaks in this way to avoid arrogance. But Luther says the other interpretation is more plausible to him, i. e., that the negative statement should be taken as an affirmative [84].

In discussing Romans 15.20 Luther states:

> "But lest we appear to completely reject the opinions of others, namely Erasmus and those who agree with him, we concede that he also strove with a certain holy ambition to be the apostle to the gentiles" [85].

In the *Hebräerbriefvorlesung* Luther continues his dialogue on certain salient points in the exegesis of Erasmus, although to a lesser degree than in the *Römerbriefvorlesung*. In his exposition of the term *reverentia* in Hebrews 5.7, Luther shows both a philological interest in the meaning of the text and a vast resource of knowledge in deriving this meaning.

> "The term *reverentia* is an ambiguous word and has several meanings ...Some (Paul of Burgos) understand it in its passive meaning as the reverence shown to Christ ... Others (Erasmus, Lefèvre) go back to the corresponding word in Greek ... Thirdly (Lyra) *reverentia* can be understood in its active sense ... Therefore this is the meaning: Christ is heard, not because we ourselves are worthy. On the contrary, we are most unworthy because of our having none of the virtue called *reverentia*. Christ is heard because his *reverentia* was worthy and of such a type that he would be heard even on behalf of the most unworthy and the highly irreverent" [86].

---

83) Ibid., 453.4. "'Analogia' enim Grece ab aliquibus 'ratio', 'comparatio', 'proportio', 'collatio', 'similitudo' dicitur, q. d. Apostolus: si vis prophetare, ita prophetes, ut fidem non excedas, ut possit fidei proprietati consonare. Quod teutonice dicitur: *Es ellicht ym. Es sihet ym gleich.*"
Cf. Erasmus, LB vi, 630. Romans 12.6.

84) WA, 56.523.30. "Quamquam non ignoro aliis Videri Apostolum id dicere pro excludenda arrogantia ... (524.3). Sed prior sensus mihil magis animo sedet, vt sit una negativa pro affirmativa; ..."

85) WA, 56.627.14. "Sed ne et aliorum reprobemus ut Erasmi et sibi similium iudicium, concedemus, quod sancta quoque ambitione quadam nisus sit Gentium Apostolus esse ..."

86) Ibid., 57.176.7. "Hoc nomen 'reverentia' ambiguum varios generat sensus ... Alii enim intelligunt passivam Christi reverentiam, ... Alli (Eras-

When expounding Hebrews 2.7 (Thou hast made him a little lower than the angels) Luther gives both a theological and a philological study that is based not only on Erasmus' annotations but also on the best of the exegetes up to and including his time:

"There are many expositors who have labored on the meaning of this verse. First, a great number of Church Fathers, notably Jerome, Ambrose, and Chrysostom, seem to understand the passage as referring to man true and simple ... Second, other expositors (Lyra and Erasmus) understand this verse to refer to Christ, that he is lower than the angels not so far as his soul is concerned but as far as the frailty of the body is concerned ... Third, Lefèvre says that in Hebrew it would say, 'Thou hast made him a little lower than *Elohim*', which means God, and not 'Thou hast made him a little lower than *malachim*', which means angels. But Erasmus disagrees with Lefèvre ... Fourth and last, Erasmus is of the opinion that the phrase 'a little lower' refers not to the measure of the diminished dignity, but to the short time during which he was made lower. The *Glossa Ordinaria* interprets the passage in this way, and also Chrysostom ... Therefore we may conclude that this verse has the same meaning as Isaiah 54.7" [87].

In summa: Luther makes extensive use of Erasmus' edition of the New Testament as a primary source book for his early exegesis, particularly in the Römerbriefvorlesung. In fact the Latin translation and the annotations of Erasmus were of considerable help to Luther as he sought to derive the real and literal meaning of the text. These examples of Luther's early exegesis also point out that he uses the philological critical method as an integral part of his exposition, although he did not always agree with Erasmus' philological conclusions or his theological assumptions.

---

mus et Lefèvre) ad Grecam equivocacionem accedunt ... Potest tercio 'reverentia' active accipi (Lyra) ... Erit ergo tunc sensus, quod Christus est exauditus, non quia nos digni eramus, imo indignissimi propter irreverentiam, sed quia sua reverentia digna fui et tanta, ut etiam pro indignissimis et irreverentissimis exaudiretur."

87) Ibid., 116.6. "A multis laboratum est in isto versu exponendo. Magna pars doctorum, precipue Hieronimus, aliquoties Augustinus, Ambrosius, Chrysostomus videntur eum de simplici humanitate intelligere ... Alii (Lyra et Erasmus) de Christo intelligunt, quod sit minor angelis non secundum animam, sed secundum corpus possibile , ... Tercio Stapulensis sic haberi dicit in Hebraeo: 'Minuist: eum paulominus ab Elohim', quod Deum significat, et non 'a Malachin', quod angelos significat. Sed huic rursus obstat Erasmus ... Quartus tandem Erasmus sentit illud 'paulominus' non referri ad modum dignitatis imminute, sed ad breve tempus, quo fuit minoratus, ut in glosa, et Chrysostomus habet ... Concluditur itaque, quod versus ille ... est eiusdem sentencie cum illo Esai. 54."

The reason, of course, that Luther could never place as much confidence as Erasmus on the philological critical method is that Luther felt that the grammatical reading must be seen first through theological eyes [88]. Erasmus saw the theory of interpretation from the directly opposite point of view, and he felt that the philological critical method of dealing with the text itself would lead to good theology. It is the case of two giants so wrapped up in their own battles that each failed to grasp the advantages of the other's point of view. Perhaps we today are poorer because of this fact.

---

88) Ibid., 5.27.8. "Primum grammatica videamus, verum ea theologica."

CONCLUSION

Erasmus' importance for his age and his influence on his period in the field of hermeneutics cannot be debated. To quote just one of many letters to Erasmus concerning his edition of the *New Testament with Annotations,*

> "I have for some months been lecturing on the Gospel of Matthew, in which I have found your elegant notes more helpful than the longer commentaries of others, especially concerning the most difficult questions" [1].

Of course, Erasmus did not always receive such praise of his edition of the New Testament, since volume nine of his *Opera Omnia* (Ed. J. Clericus) is filled with various defenses of his work, but nevertheless Erasmus seems to have been read, if not always appreciated.

Any great man will make good friends and strong enemies, and Erasmus is no exception. His primary aim was the restoration of the Biblical text, and this in itself, especially in his age, was sufficient ground for criticism. Erasmus' life work is an attempt to break with the established order and his hermeneutic exemplifies this attempt. To summarize his hermeneutic illustrates his departure from the scholastic method of interpretation.

The formal principle of Erasmus' hermeneutic is an erudite attempt to deal with the sources themselves, and the authority of the sources is determined by their merit in relation to the philosophy of Christ.

The method and key to his goal was the philological critical method, implemented by an historical critical approach. For this

---

1) Allen, 579.22. From Henry Bullock. "Professus sum per menses aliquot Euangelium Matthei, in quo plus his tuis elagantissimis annotationculis quam longissimis non nullorum commentariis sum adiutus, in nobis praesertim difficilioribus."

reason it can be said that Erasmus was a forerunner of both textual and historical criticism[2].

One question remains to be answered. We have said that Erasmus differed in method from the scholastic approach and that he is a precursor of today's method. Then what is his relation to the Reformation? As the editor of the New Testament text and in his philological critical approach to the text of the New Testament, Erasmus gave to the Reformation the text and method that were so important for their theological exegesis of the text.

Hermann Schlingensiepen has said that "Die transzendente Grundlage des Christentums bleibt unangetastet durch ihn"[3]. But Erasmus is more than a transcendent force in the field of hermeneutics, for in his hermeneutic are all the elements that we now use and take for granted, but that Erasmus struggled to promote.

Lastly, what does the hermeneutic of Erasmus say to the present hermeneutical debate? Ersamus was primarily interested in method and it was this emphasis that sharpened the controversy with Luther, who was more interested in meaning. And again today, is the "New Hermeneutic" more concerned with method than the meaning that lies behind that method?

The fact remains that a hermeneutical weakness is inherent in Erasmus' principle of erudition, as Luther pointed out in his *De servum arbitrium*. And is not the present discussion in hermeneutics also, although in a different sense, centered on erudition and man's understanding? It was Luther's contention in his concept of *spiritus* that the Word of God breaks through to us of its own accord. This is also Karl Barth's thesis in his "Preface to the First Edition of the Römerbrief". And in the doctrine of interpretation it is this point that must remain central. The basic criterion of any hermeneutic must be the content of the revelation itself rather than the means and methods of achieving understanding of that revelation.

---

2) RGG VI, 717. Greeven, H., "Text und Textkritik der Bibel II. Neues Testament." "Die Geschichte der wissenschaftlichen Textkritik des Neues Testament beginnt damit, dass man die weitverbreitete, von Erasmus besorgte Erstausgabe des griech. Neues Testament."

3) "Erasmus als Exeget. Auf Grund seiner Schriften zu Matthäus," *Zeitschrift für Kirchengeschichte* 48. Gotha, 1929, p. 56.

PRIMARY SOURCES

Allen   — *Opus Epistolarum Erasmi*, ed. Percy S. and H. M. Allen, 11 vols., Oxford, 1906—47. (Cited by number and line of the letter).

CR   — *Corpus Reformatorum* (Calvin's Works), ed. Baum, Cunitz and Reuss., Vols. 1—59, Brunswick, 1863—1900.

Froben   — *Des. Erasmi Roter. Opervm.* "Sectuvs Tomvs-Novvm Testamentum", ed. Boniface Amerbach, Froben, Basel.

Holborn   — *Desiderius Erasmus Roterodamus, Ausgewählte Werke*, ed. Hoja and Annemarie Holborn. München, 1933. *(Enchiridion Militis Christiani, In N. T. Praefationes, Ratio ... ad veram Theologiam).*

Inst.   — Calvin, *Institutio Christianae Religionis*. Geneva 1559. (CR Vol. XXX OS Vols. 3—5).

LB   — *Desiderii Erasmi Roterdami Opera Omnia*, ed. J. Clericus, Leiden. 11 vols., 1703—16. (cited by vol., page and section).

Opuscula   — *Erasmi Opuscula, a supplement to the Opera Omnia*, ed. W. K. Ferguson. The Hague, 1933. (Poems, *Julius exclusus e coelis*, etc.).

OS   — *Calvini Opera Selecta*, ed. Peter Barth and Wilhelm Niesel, Vols. 1—5, Munich, 1926—1952.

WA   — *D. Martin Luthers Werke*, Weimarer Ausgabe, Weimar, 1883—1939.

BIBLIOGRAPHY

Aland, Kurt: *Kirchengeschichtliche Entwürfe*. Berlin, 1960.

Atkinson, James: *Luther: Early Theological Works* (The Library of Christian Classics, Vol. XVI). London, 1953.

Bainton, Roland H.: *Here I Stand, a life of Martin Luther*. New York, 1950.

— "Renaissance und Religion", *Die Religion in Geschichte und Gegenwart*, ed. V, pp. 1059—1063. 3rd Edition, Tübingen, 1957—62.

Barth, Karl: *Die Kirchliche Dogmatik*, I—IV. Zürich, 1932—59.

Berger, Samuel: *La Bible au Seizième Siècle*. Paris, 1879.

Bibliotheca Erasmiana, Repertoire des oeuvres d'Erasme, listes sommaires. Gand, 1893.

Binns, Leonard E.: *Erasmus, the Reformer*. London, 1928.

Bludau, Aug.: *Die beiden ersten Erasmus-Ausgaben des N. T. (Biblische Studien*, VII. Band, 5. Heft) Freiburg im Breisgau, 1902.

Bohatec, Josef: *Bude und Calvin*. Wien, 1950.

Bouyer, Louis: *Autour d'Erasme. Etudes sur le christianisme des humanistes catholiques*. Paris, 1955.

Cadier, Jean: *Calvin, L'homme que Dieu a dompté*. Geneva, 1958.

Cambell, William: *Erasmus, Tyndale, and More*. London, 1949.

Chambers, R. W.: *Thomas More*. London, 1935.

Cullmann, Oscar: *Die Christologia des Neuen Testaments*, Tübingen, 1957.

Drummond, R. B.: *Erasmus: his life and character as shown in his correspondence and works*. 2 vols., London, 1873.

Ebeling, Gerhard: *Evangelische Evangelien Auslegung. Eine Untersuchung zu Luthers Hermeneutik*. München, 1942.

— "Hermeneutik", *Die Religion in Geschichte und Gegenwart*, Band III, pp. 242—262. 3rd Edition, Tübingen, 1957—62.

— *Kirchengeschichte als Geschichte der Auslegung der Heiligen Schrift*. Tübingen, 1947.

Froude, J. A.: *Life and Letters of Erasmus*. London, 1895.

Fuchs, Ernst: *Zum Hermeneutischen Problem in der Theologie. Die existentiale Interpretation*. Tübingen, 1959.

Gedenkschrift zum 400. Todestage des Erasmus von Rotterdam. Basel, 1936. Allen, Percy Stafford, "The Young Erasmus". Hartmann, Alfred, "Beatus

Rhenanus: Leben und Werke des Erasmus". Kaegi, Werner, "Erasmus im achtzehnten Jahrhundert". Major, Emil, "Die Grabstätte des Erasmus". Pfeiffer, Rudolf, "Die Wandlungen der 'Antibarbari'". Rüegg, August, "Des Erasmus 'Lob der Torheit' und Thomas Morus 'Utopia'". Staehelin, Ernst, "Erasmus u. Oekolampad in ihrem Ringen um die Kirche Jesu Christi".

Gibbon, Edward: *The Decline and Fall of the Roman Empire.* London, 1776.

Gilmore, M. P.: *The World of Humanism* (1453—1517). New York, 1952.

Grass, Hans: (Ausgewählt u. eingeleitet) *Quellen zur Konfessions-Kunde.* Heft 1. "Die Katholische Lehre von der heiligen Schrift und von der Tradition". Lüneburg, 1954.

Greeven, H.: "Text und Textkritik der Bibel II. Neues Testament", *Die Religion in Geschichte und Gegenwart*, Band VI, pp. 715—724, 3rd Edition, Tübingen, 1957—62.

Haroutunian, Joseph: (ed. and translator) and Smith, Louis Pettibone, *Calvin: Commentaries* (The Library of Christian Classics, Vol. XVIII) London, 1958.

Holl, Karl: *Gesammelte Aufsätze zur Kirchengeschichte.* Vol. 1, "Luther". Tübingen, 1921.

Hudson, Hoyt Hopewell: trans., *The Praise of Folly.* Princeton, 1947.

Huizinga, J.: *Erasmus.* Deutsch von Werner Kaegi. Basel, 1951.

Hyma, Albert: "The Youth of Erasmus", (Vol. 10, *History and Political Science*). Ann Arbor, 1930.

Johnson, E.: ed., *Familiar Colloquies,* N. Bailey, trans., 3 vols., London, 1900.

Jortin, J.: *The Life of Erasmus.* 2 vols., London, 1758—60.

Knight, Samuel: *The Life of Erasmus.* London, 1726.

Köhler, Walther: ed., *Erasmus von Rotterdam Briefe.* Würzburg, 1956.

Kropatschekh, Friedrich: *Das Schriftprinzip der lutherischen Kirche.* Band I, "Die Vorgeschichte. Das Erbe des Mittelalters". Leipzig, 1904.

Kümmel, W. G.: "Bibelwissenschaft des Neutestaments", *Die Religion in Geschichte und Gegenwart*, Bd. I, pg. 1235—1251. 3rd. Edition, Tübingen, 1957.

— *Das Neue Testament. Geschichte der Erforschung seiner Probleme.* München, 1958.

Leipoldt, Johannes, *Geschichte des neutestamentlichen Kanons,* 2 vols., Leipzig, 1907—8.

Major, Emil: "Erasmus von Rotterdam", *(Virorum Illustrium Reliquiae I),* Basel, 1925.

Mangan, John Joseph: *Erasmus, Life, Character, and Influence.* 2 vols., New York, 1925.

Maurer, Wilhelm: "Luthers Verständnis des neutestamentlichen Kanons", *Fuldaer Hefte.* Berlin, 1960.

Meissinger, Karl A.: *Erasmus von Rotterdam.* Zürich, 1942.

Mestwerdt, P.: "Die Anfänge des Erasmus, Humanismus und Devotio Moderna", (*Studien zur Kultur und Geschichte der Reformation II*). Leipzig, 1917.

Murray, Robert H.: *Erasmus and Luther: Their attitude toward Toleration.* New York and London, 1920.

Nichols, F. W.: *The Epistles of Erasmus from his earliest years to his 53rd year.* 3 vols., London, 1907—18.

Niesel, Wilhelm: *Die Theologie Calvins.* München, 1938.

Nolhac, Pierre de: *Erasme en Italie.* Paris, 1898.

Noltensmeier, Hermann: *Das Schriftverständnis bei Luther und Calvin.* Graz-Köln, 1953.

Østergaard-Nielsen, Harold: *Scriptura sacra et viva vox.* München, 1957.

Padberg, Rudolf: *Erasmus als Katechet.* Freiburg, 1956.

Pauk, Wilhelm: *Luther: Lectures on Romans* (The Library of Christian Classics, Vol. XIV). London, 1953.

Phillips, Margaret Mann: *Erasmus and the Northern Renaissance.* London, 1949.

Pineau, J.: *Erasme, sa pensée religieuse.* Paris, 1924.

Renaudet, Augustin: *Études erasmiennes* (1521—9). Paris, 1939.

— *Erasme, Sa pensée religieuse* (1518—21). (Bibliothèque de la Revue historique). Paris, 1926.

Reedijk, Cornelis: *The Poems of Desiderius Erasmus (Erasmus Carmina).* Leiden, 1956.

Reid, J. K. S.: *The Authority of Scripture: A Study of Reformation and Post-Reformation Understanding of the Bible.* London, 1957.

Ritter, Gerhard: *Die Neugestaltung Europas im 16. Jh.* Berlin, 1950.

Rügg, W.: *Cicero und der Humanismus.* Zürich, 1946.

— "Humanismus", *Die Religion in Geschichte und Gegenwart* II. Philosophisch, Band III, pp. 479—482. Tübingen, 1957—62.

Santillana, Giorgio de: *The Age of Adventure. The Renaissance Philosophers.* (Mentor edition). New York, 1956.

Schaff, Philip: *The Creeds of Christendom.* London and New York, 1877.

Schiel, Hubert: *Übertragen und Eingeleitet von: Handbüchlein des christlichen Streiters.* Olten und Freiburg im Breisgau, 1952.

Schlechta, Karl: *Erasmus von Rotterdam.* Hamburg, 1940.

Schlingensiepen, Hermann: *Erasmus als Exeget. Auf Grund seiner Schriften zu Matthäus.* (Zeitschrift für Kirchengeschichte 48, pp. 16—47). Gotha, 1929.

Schottenloher, O.: "Erasmus", *Die Religion in Geschichte und Gegenwart*, Band II, pp. 534—537, 3rd. Edition, Tübingen, 1957—62.

Seeberg, Erich: *Luthers Theologie, Motive und Ideen.* Vol. I, Göttingen, 1929; Vol. II, Stuttgart, 1937.

Seebohm, Frederic: *The Oxford Reformers. John Colet, Erasmus, and Thomas More.* 3rd. Edition, London, 1887.

Smalley, Beryl: *The Study of the Bible in the Middle Ages.* Oxford, 1952.

Smart, James D.: *The Interpretation of Scripture.* Philadelphia, 1961.

Smith, Preserved: *A Key to the Colloquies of Erasmus* (Harvard Theological Studies). Cambridge (USA), 1927.

— *Erasmus, a study in his life, ideals and place in history.* New York and London, 1923.

Spicq, P. C.: *Esquisse D'une Histoire De L'exégèse Latinae au Moyen Age.* (Bibliothèque Thomiste). Paris, 1944.

Spinka, Matthew: *Advocates of Reform, from Wyclif to Erasmus.* (The Library of Christian Classics, Vol. XIV). London, 1953.

Stupperich, R.: "Humanismus", *Die Religion in Geschichte und Gegenwart.* I Historisch, Band III, pp. 478—479. 3rd edition, Tübingen, 1957—1962.

Thompson, Craig R., ed.: *Colloquia Familiaria.* (The Library of Liberal Arts, No. 48). New York, 1957.

— *Inquisito de Fide. A Colloquy by Desiderius Erasmus* 1524. (Yale Studies in Religion XV). London, 1950.

Treu, Erwin: *Die Bildnisse des Erasmus von Rotterdam.* Basel, 1959.

Wernle, Paul: *Die Renaissance des Christentums im 16. Jh.* Tübingen, Leipzig, 1940.